Humanizing Big Data

Marketing at the meeting of data, social science and consumer insight

Colin Strong

KoganPage

LONDON PHILADELPHIA NEW DELHI

First published in Great Britain and the United States in 2015 by Kogan Page Limited

2nd Floor, 45 Gee Street	1518 Walnut Street, Suite 1100	4737/23 Ansari Road
London EC1V 3RS	Philadelphia PA 19102	Daryaganj
United Kingdom	USA	New Delhi 110002
		India

www.koganpage.com

© Colin Strong, 2015

The right of Colin Strong to be identified as the author of this work has been asserted by him in accordance with the Copyright, Designs and Patents Act 1988.

ISBN   978 0 7494 7211 5
E-ISBN   978 0 7494 7212 2

British Library Cataloguing-in-Publication Data

A CIP record for this book is available from the British Library.

Library of Congress Cataloging-in-Publication Data

CIP data is available.

Library of Congress Control Number: 2015000570

Typeset by Amnet
Print production managed by Jellyfish
Printed and bound by CPI Group (UK) Ltd, Croydon, CR0 4YY

CONTENTS

PART TWO Smart thinking 91

PART THREE Consumer thinking

11   Off limits?

12   Getting personal

13   Privacy paradox

PREFACE

It will not have gone unnoticed by anyone involved in big data that the debate about it has become increasingly polarized. On the one hand there are strong advocates of its value who see it as fundamentally changing not only how we do business but the way in which science and indeed the world we inhabit is organized. At the other end of the spectrum are sceptics who consider it is over-hyped and does not fundamentally change anything.

This book contributes to the debate because it is concerned with the way in which brands use big data for marketing purposes. As such it is a book about human beings – our ability to make sense of data, to derive new meanings from it and our experience of living in a data-mediated world. There is inevitably spill-over into other areas but that is what the core of this book is about. Much of what the book contains will be relevant to non-profit organizations and government agencies but for the sake of simplicity the key point of reference is to brands.

Of course, the case for big data has, at times, inevitably been some-what overstated. Technologists are generally the most guilty of this, with their perspective often being infused with a sense that if only we can reduce all human behaviour to a series of data points then we will be able to predict much of our future activity. This reductionist view of human behaviour fails to recognize the complexity of the world in which we live, the subtle eco-systems we inhabit and the context in which behaviours take place. A reductionist use of big data, certainly in the context of personal data, means that the marketing profession is in danger of reducing its remit, becoming a tactical rather than strategic part of the organization.

The sceptics on the other hand are not seeing the case for the potential value that lies in big data. We have a massive resource available to us that tracks our behaviours in a manner so thorough, so intimate and so consistent that it is hard not to see that there must surely be gold in those hills. The question is what is it and how do we find a way to get it?

This book is about how marketers can recapture the big data agenda, wrestling it away from technologists and reasserting a more strategic viewpoint. Doing so will surely reinvigorate the marketing profession. Understanding data relating to human behaviour is a long-standing skill of marketers and social scientists. We are starting to see that many of their practitioner skills that help us read and interpret data are just as valid in a big data world. New challenges are of course thrown up but this just means that we need to think about these issues in original ways.

We can derive so much from our data trails yet a lot of the analysis and interpretation remains at a pretty basic behavioural level. As brands struggle to find differentiation in a world where technology reduces their ability to stand out from the competition, then this creates an opportunity. Human behaviour is complex but big data offers new ways to understand that complexity. And complexity should be the friend of the marketer as this provides opportunities to find differences to leverage.

Social scientists are often ahead of brands on exploiting the opportunities that can be found in big data. New fields such as cyber psychology, computational sociology and cultural analytics are emerging which make good use of big data and heightened computing power to generate new insights into human behaviour. It is to these new fields that brands can look to find new ways to search for meaning in the morass of data.

And in the midst of all this we cannot forget the experience of the consumer. For it is the consumer that is producing this data but also then being the recipient of activities borne from that very data. Is the consumer a willing participant in this? We need to explore the ways consumers understand their experience as these issues, such as privacy and empowerment, are themselves rapidly becoming a source of differentiation for brands.

This book is not a detailed 'how to' book, although there is hopefully a lot of useful guidance contained within it. Rather it is a call to arms to seize the opportunity to see how big data can be used to understand consumers in new and exciting ways. At its heart is the point that in order to be smart about big data, we really need to understand humans. We cannot interpret data without understanding the pitfalls we can potentially fall into in the process. We need frameworks of behaviour to help us explore data sets. We need to understand how humans react to data-mediated environments to understand how brands can best implement data strategies.

The book is a manifesto for brands to think differently about data. In the process you may start to see humans differently. It is designed to set people thinking and spark debate. Thank you for picking this up and being part of that.

ACKNOWLEDGEMENTS

There are a number of people and organizations that I need to thank for their support. First, my wife Joanne, for her support and her inspiration across the breadth of topics in the book. Second, I would like to thank my colleagues and friends who have discussed and reviewed the material and thinking with me. Particular thanks are owed to Dr Guy Champniss, Stuart Crawford Browne, Ryan Garner, Alan Mitchell, Corrine Moy, Anders Nielsen, Simon Pulman Jones and Iain Stanfield.

I am also very grateful to Henry Stuart Publications for allowing me to use a version of a paper that appeared in *Applied Marketing Analytics* for Chapter 12. Similarly, I am grateful to IOS Press for allowing me to use a version of a paper that appeared in the *Digital Enlightenment Yearbook 2014* for Chapter 11. I would like to thank Simon Pulman Jones for allowing me to use the content of a paper on which we collaborated on for the 2013 Market Research Society Conference entitled 'Visual awareness: A manifesto for market research to engage with the language of images' as a basis for some of the content in Chapter 9. My thanks to Stuart Crawford Browne for the contributions he made to earlier versions of the book.

To Joanne, although she would have preferred a book of love sonnets.

This changes everything

Throughout history, mankind's progress has been driven by our ability to devise new technologies. Agriculture is a good example. Between the 8th and the 18th centuries, the technology involved in farming more or less stayed the same and few advances were achieved. So a UK farmer in the 18th century was effectively using the same kit as a farmer in Julius Caesar's day.

Then in the mid-1700s James Small created the first effective single-furrow horse plough, which hugely increased efficiency. A number of other advances were made at that time, such as Jethro Tull's seed drill. These had a major impact on the UK's ability to support a growing population, which grew to record levels. This, in turn, led to greater demand for goods and services as well as a new class of landless labourer, effectively creating the conditions for the Industrial Revolution.

Technology, as Nicolas Carr points out in his excellent book, *The Shallows*,[1] reflects and shapes the way in which we understand the world. For instance, the mechanical clock changed the way we saw ourselves. The clock defined time in terms of units of equal duration, so we were able to start comprehending the concepts of division and measurement. We began to see, in the world around us, how the whole is composed of individual pieces that are in turn themselves composed of pieces. We began to understand that there are abstract patterns behind the visible appearance of the material world. And this mindset effectively propelled us out of the Middle Ages, into the Renaissance and then the Enlightenment.

The tools we are using will always shape our understanding, so if our tools suddenly grow and change then so will our capacity to understand the world. Information technology is having just such an impact, although we have not yet properly understood how it will change the way we understand the world. Technology now allows us to measure the world with an ease never before imagined.

As Kenneth Cukier and Viktor Mayer-Schönberger suggest in their book *Big Data: A revolution that will transform how we live, work and think*,[2] the world is increasingly becoming 'datafied'. By this, they mean putting a natural phenomenon in a quantified format so it can be tabulated and analysed. As humans we have always attempted to datafy the world – think mapping, scientific experiments, weather forecasting or censuses. But what has changed is the degree to which modern IT system have facilitated this process. IT fundamentally alters our ability to quantify the world both through the way in which phenomena are now effectively transformed into data but also via our ability to store and then make sense of that information.

To date, much of what has been datafied is in the physical domain but we are now at the point where much of human behaviour is now being 'datafied'. We have perhaps not yet properly considered the implications of this for our understanding of human behaviour but they are undoubtedly enormous. Previously we have had to rely on a wide variety of interventions in order to measure and understand human behaviour. We have placed people in laboratories and looked to see how they operate under controlled conditions. We have asked people survey questions to elicit their insights into their behaviours and attitudes. We have attached electrodes to track the inner workings of their brain. We may give them life-logging tools that record their day to day activity. We visit people's homes to better understand how they live. We gather people into viewing studios to talk about their experiences. There is an endless stream of ingenious ways in which we aim to better understand ourselves and our fellow human beings.

But now we have a new set of tools. As our lives become increasingly datafied we are able to explore what people actually *do* rather than what they *say they do*. New sources of data tell us what people are doing in an incredibly granular and intimate way. And not only does it tell us what people are doing but, as we shall see later, this data also reveals what people are thinking, what is *shaping* their behaviour. Compare this with the rudimentary materials available to the early psychologists such as Hans Eysenck,[3] who researched wounded soldiers in World War II for his work on personality. If Eysenck were still alive today, he would surely be very excited by the massive new data sources we have available to conduct research. Not only does it make existing research potentially much easier to undertake but it also creates the opportunity for fundamentally new insights into human behaviour.

Academics have not been slow to recognize this potential. As Scott Golder, one of an emerging breed of computational sociologists says:[4]

> What is new is the macroscopic global scale and microscopic behavioural extensiveness of the data that is becoming available for social and behavioural science. The web sees everything and forgets nothing. Each click and key press resides in a data warehouse waiting to be mined for insights into behaviour.

And of course there is no shortage of data available for us to examine. As the 21st century came into being and our IT systems were not killed off by the millennium bug after all, the amount of data mankind collected started to radically grow. Paul Zikopoulos *et al*[5] reported that in the year 2000 about 800,000 petabytes of data were stored in the world. This has simply exploded so that by 2010 it was 'estimated that enterprises globally stored more than seven exabytes of new data on disk drives... while consumers stored more than six exabytes of new data on devices such as PCs and notebooks.'[6] Hal Varian, Chief Economist at Google (cited in Smolan and Erwitt 2012),[7] estimates that humankind now produces the same amount of data in any two days than in all of history prior to 2003. There is simply no shortage of data.

This book is about the opportunities for brands that lie in using these huge data assets to get a better understanding of human behaviour. Of course, organizations are increasingly using data to transform all aspects of their business, including transforming their operational processes, customer experience and ultimately changing business models.[8] But this book is specifically about the way in which brands can create real competitive advantage through the use of data for consumer understanding.

Through the use of digital technology, a small start-up can now rapidly position themselves as key competitors to large corporates. The computer manufacturer ASUS is a good example of this. In their book, *Absolute Value*,[9] authors Itamar Simonson and Emanuel Rosen tell how a good product with competitive pricing can succeed through clever use of social media and not require huge investment in advertising. And of course, digital technology now means that it is easier than ever to manage off-shoring of production, sales processes, customer service etc. So there are forces for increasing homogenization of businesses. Increasingly the one source of differentiation is consumer understanding. At one level data levels the playing field, lowering the barriers to entry, allowing small brands to quickly start competing against established businesses. On the other hand it provides new opportunities for smart organizations to understand their consumers in new ways and therefore create strategies that offer much needed differentiation in the market.

The breadth and depth of datafication

There are a wide range of ways in which our lives are becoming increasingly 'datafied', so that we are unwittingly revealing a huge amount about ourselves in the process. Some of the ways in which our lives are becoming increasingly datafied are outlined below.

Datafication of sentiment/emotions

The explosion of self-reporting on social media has led us to provide very intimate details of ourselves. For example, with billions of people now using Facebook and Twitter, we have an incredible database of how people are feeling. Many market research companies use this by 'scraping' the web to obtain detailed information on the sentiment relating to particular issues, often brands, products and services.

Datafication of interactions/relationships

We are now not only able to see the ways in which people relate but with whom they relate. So again, social media has transformed our understanding of relationships by datafying professional and personal connections. Historically, our ability to collect relational data has necessarily been through direct contact and therefore this has generally limited studies of social interactions to small groups such as clubs and villages. Social media now allows us to explore relationships on a global scale.

Datafication of speech

It is not just the written word or connections that have come within the ambit of datafication. Speech analytics is becoming more common, particularly as conversations are increasingly recorded and stored as part of interaction with call centres. As speech recognition improves, the range of voice-based data that can be captured in an intelligible format can only grow. Call centres are the most obvious beneficiaries of speech analytics, particularly when overlaid with other data. They can be used to identify why people call, improve resolution rates, ensure that those who answer a call follow their script, improve the performance of call centre employees, increase sales and identify problems.

Datafication of what is traditionally seen as offline activity

Within many data-intensive industries such as finance, healthcare and e-commerce there is a huge amount of data available on individual behaviours and outcomes. But there is also a growing awareness of the potential to utilize big data approaches in traditionally non-digital spheres. For example, retailers have been gathering enormous amounts of data from their online offerings but have struggled to do the same in their bricks-and-mortar stores.

That is changing through innovations such as image analysis of in-store cameras to monitor traffic patterns, tracking positions of shoppers from mobile phone signals, and the use of shopping cart transponders and RFID (radio-frequency identification). When overlaid with transactional and lifestyle information it becomes the basis of encouraging loyalty and targeting promotions.

Facial recognition software is also growing more sophisticated. For example, companies have developed software that can map emotional responses to a greater degree of sensitivity than ever before.[10] In the UK, supermarket giant Tesco has even been experimenting with installing TV-style screens above the tills in a number of its petrol stations. They scan the eyes of customers to determine age and gender, and then run tailored advertisements. The technology also adjusts messages depending on the time and date, as well as monitoring customer purchases.[11]

Datafication of culture

We are increasingly able to convert cultural artefacts into data, generating new insights into the way in which our culture has changed over time. The new discipline of 'cultural analytics' typically uses digital image processing and visualization for the exploratory analysis of image and video collections to explore these cultural trends. Google's Ngram service, the datafication of over 5.2 million of the world's books from between the years 1800 and 2000, is perhaps the largest-scale example of just such a project.

These are just some of the ways in which many of our behaviours that have previously not been available to big data analytics are now open to measurement and analysis in ways never before imagined. But perhaps we need to step back a moment and consider; what is it that we are actually gathering here? What does 'data' actually consist of? It's an easy term to use but is perhaps a little harder to actually define.

What is data?

The word 'data' is actually derived from the Latin *dare*, meaning 'to give'. So originally the meaning of data was that which can be 'given by' a phenomenon. However, as commentator Rob Kitchin points out,[12] in general use, 'data' refers to those elements that are taken; extracted through observations, computations, experiments, and record-keeping.[13]

So what we understand as data are actually 'capta' (derived from the Latin *capere*, meaning 'to take'); those units of data that have been selected and harvested from the sum of all potential data. So, as Kitchin suggests, it is perhaps an accident of history that the term datum and not captum has come to symbolize the unit in science. On this basis, science does not deal with 'that which has been given' by nature to the scientist, but with 'that which has been taken', that is selected from nature by the scientist based on what it is needed for.

What this brief discussion starts to highlight is that data harvested through measurement is always a selection from the total sum of all possible data available – what we have chosen to take from all that could potentially be given. As such, data is inherently partial, selective and representative.

And this is one of the key issues in this book that we will return to again and again. The way we use data is a series of choices and as such the data does not 'speak for itself'. If we want to make sense of all this data then we need to understand the lens through which we are looking at it.

Defining big data

There has been so much written about big data elsewhere that there is little point in dwelling on definitions. However, it is worth mentioning the way in which different elements of the generally agreed understanding of what we mean by big data have relevance to furthering our understanding of human behaviour.

There is no single agreed academic or industry definition of big data, but a survey by Rob Kitchin[14] of the emerging literature identifies a number of key features. Big data is:

- huge in *volume* – allowing us to explore the breadth of human behaviour;

- high in *velocity*, created in or near real-time – allowing us to see how behaviours are being formed in the moment;

- diverse in *variety*, including both structured and unstructured data – reflecting the way in which we can draw on various data sets to reflect the diversity of contexts of human behaviours;

- *exhaustive* in scope, often capturing entire populations or systems – facilitating an understanding of the diversity of human behaviour;

- fine-grained in *resolution* – allowing us to understand very granular, intimate behaviours;

- *relational* in nature – facilitating new insights given that much of our behaviour is context-dependent;

- *flexible*, so we can add new fields easily and we can expand the scope rapidly – allowing a resource that can be continually developed and mined for new insights.

Qualities of big data

It is worth thinking more about the properties of big data in the context of what opportunities it affords the marketer, or more likely the market researcher that is supporting this function in an organization. Drawing on the thinking of Scott Golder and Michael Macy,[15] the points below highlight the new opportunities that big data can start to deliver.

Social data

Our lives can be hard to observe, particularly when we want to understand the social aspects of how we live. In the past if we wanted to understand how relationships worked we would have to ask an individual person about their family and friends. This was by necessity very limiting so we could only explore social ties in small groups or communities and then for limited periods of time. Researchers are faced with a Hobson's choice. On the one hand there is the statistically robust representative study that involves random samples of individuals selected to be an unbiased representation of the underlying population. But here we have nothing to help us understand the effect of the respondents' social ties versus their own individual traits.

On the other hand we have methodologies such as snowball sampling which can be used to find connections from that original respondent, but has the negative impact of it being difficult to obtain a properly unbiased representation of the underlying population using this means.

Access to big data resolves this as it gives opportunity to examine social relationships without having to use the constraints of previous methodologies (which have the effect of implicitly assuming that behaviours are fundamentally determined by individual characteristics). We can now properly examine the nature of social relationships by examining our data trails in all their glory. The frequency and intensity of our social relationships are laid out in a way that has never before been seen.

Longitudinal data

Longitudinal data is the gold standard for any social science researcher. Understanding how a consumer operates over time across different contexts is enormously valuable. But obtaining the data is expensive. Market research organizations will typically have large-scale panels of consumers that they have recruited, tracking a huge range of consumer-related activities, attitudes and intentions. Governments also invest in the collection of time series data to study health and welfare issues and will involve a range of government, market research and academic bodies to co-ordinate the challenging logistics of the task. But gathering longitudinal data remains an expensive operation. Now, however, the use of big data allows us to look at the way in which individuals behave (and as we shall see later, think), to see what activity led up to a particular event that is of interest and indeed when particular behaviours did not result in an outcome of interest. Big data has the potential to transform our ability to look at behaviour over time.

Breadth of data

As Scott Golder and Michael Macy point out, 'The web sees everything and forgets nothing'. Whilst we would use the term big data rather than the web, this means that we now have access to a world of immensely granular information about our lives that we could not hope to collect in any other way, both from the internet but also from huge data banks owned by governments and corporates. So we can get access to both the very large phenomena (such as the way in which social effects might influence social unrest) through to intimate and granular footage of our lives (such as the frequency by which we drink or do housework).

Real-time data

We now have access to data that is recorded in real time rather than, as has historically been the case, collected retrospectively. We know that asking respondents to recall their past activity has limited value in some contexts. So, for example, there are limits to the accuracy of recall when asking for very detailed information of past experiences. Big data means we can see exactly when each activity has taken place and, where relevant, with whom and what was communicated. Survey data is still important but we are starting to see that it has a new role in the era of big data.

Unobtrusive data

Big data is collected 'passively', that is the respondent does not need to be engaged in the process, as is the case for surveys for example. As such this limits the potential for design effects where the respondent changes their behaviour as a function of the intervention. This could be that the respondent goes about their activity or reports it in a way that reflects what they would like us believe – or indeed what they believe they typically do – but does not necessarily reflect the reality of their typical routine.

Retrospective data

Online interactions have been described as 'persistent conversations'.[16] So unlike in-person conversations and transactions, digital activity can be recorded with perfect accuracy and indeed persists forever. So although we need to take care to understand the context in which the conversation took place, it can be reconstructed allowing retrospective analysis to be very complete and precise compared to other means we have for retrospective analysis of events.

So there are many ways in which these new data sources are providing marketers with fundamentally new opportunities for insights. And this is not to say that these should replace other methods such as surveys, as each can be used to provide information that is missing in the other. So, for example, surveys are able to provide very reliable estimates of the way in which attitudes are distributed in the population but can often only provide retrospective (although more real-time options are now being used) responses, do not allow us to properly understand the effect of social relationships and of course are subject to the respondent's own ability to report their internal state.

This book

Data seems to have a strange effect on many people. It is approached with a certain awe and reverence as if it is telling immutable truths that cannot be questioned. This book sets out to question this mindset but more positively seeks to explore the way in which we can derive a greater understanding of the human condition through data.

Part One of the book explores how we read data and is effectively a call to arms to apply critical thinking to the data that we collect from IT systems. The data itself is not fallible but how we choose to collect it, scrutinize and make sense of it certainly is. A critical discussion is then undertaken of two key areas in which big data is considered to have significant importance – prediction and advertising. The point of these chapters is not to say that prediction and advertising are not enhanced by the availability of data, rather that there are all manner of traps that we can fall into if we fail to think critically when we use data.

Part Two of the book provides an alternative to the widespread assumption that big data 'speaks for itself', that all we need to do to generate real insight from that data is to stand back and allow it to reveal its insights. As the reader will see in Part One, we cannot rely on correlations alone; we need to use frameworks of human behaviour to facilitate the way in which we explore that data. We are in rather a strange position at the moment where analysis of consumer understanding from big data is typically in the hands of technologists rather than social scientists. At one level this is understandable, given the tools to manipulate this are technology driven. But this seems a feeble explanation that is resulting in a very pale imitation of what it is to be a human. Reductionist models of human behaviour abound. It is time for marketers to reclaim their territory, working with technologists to facilitate the way in which brands can generate differentiation in their understanding of human behaviour. In this section of the book we also touch on the way in which technology allows us to explore how a wider community can be called upon to engage in this activity. No longer is data analytics the preserve of a small elite, whether technologists or social scientists. It serves an organization well to call upon a broad range of perspectives and skill sets, which new technology platforms now easily facilitate.

The final section of the book is about the experience of the consumer in a data-mediated world. As brands are increasingly 'digitally transformed', their relationship with consumers is increasingly through the use of data. So consumers may be targeted by digital advertising, viewing and purchasing of goods is conducted online, the customer touch-points of an organization are often via digital initiatives, and indeed the services themselves may be digital services.

How does the consumer feel about this? There is a generally held assumption that managing consumer relationships in this way is a good thing and will inevitably lead to business growth. Indeed a survey by consulting firm Capgemini[17] found business executives considered big data would improve business performance by 41 per cent over a three-year period, reflecting the optimism held about the promise of big data. But is the relationship between productivity and big data always a linear one? In Part Three we suggest that this is not necessarily the case; the relationship is in fact more complex with, for example, consumers falling into an 'uncanny valley' if they experience too much data-driven personalized advertising.

The use of data is throwing up big questions for brands in terms of consumer empowerment, privacy and personalization. The questions here can feel at odds with the popular sentiment revolving around big data. Yet perhaps the initial hubris of what big data can achieve is starting to pass and we are entering a new phase of realism, where we start to be pragmatic about what is possible. But also more excited, certainly in the area of consumer understanding, as the issues become more thoughtful and nuanced.

There is a huge opportunity for brands to make use of big data but it requires a change of mindset. There are many vested interests that have talked about the potential of big data but in a way that maintains a simplistic approach to consumer understanding: allowing the data to 'speak for itself' rather than thinking about what it means; accepting reductionist views of human behaviour rather than recognizing that a higher-level order of explanation is often needed; using a range of data-derived metrics simply because you can, not because they mean anything; implementing customer management programmes that are efficient because they are data-mediated but not considering the impact on the brand. The list goes on. But those brands that take the challenge set out in this book will find that there are ways in which data transformation does not need to be a race to homogeneity, but the start of a nuanced understanding of the way in which differentiation is possible.

Notes

1 Carr, Nicholas (2011) *The Shallows: How the internet is changing the way we think, read and remember*, Atlantic Books

2 Cukier, Kenneth and Mayer-Schönberger, Viktor (2013) *Big Data: A revolution that will transform how we live, work and think*, John Murray

3 Eyesenck, Jans J (1997) *Rebel With a Cause: The autobiography of Hans Eyesenck*, Transaction Publishers

4 Golder, Scott A and Macy, Michael W (2014) Digital footprints: opportunities and challenges for online social research, *Annual Review of Sociology* 40, pp 129–52

5 Zikopoulos, P, Eaton, C, deRoos, D, Deutsch, T and Lapis, G (2012) *Understanding Big Data*, McGraw Hill, New York

6 Manyika, J, Chiu, M, Brown, B, Bughin, J, Dobbs, R, Roxburgh, C and Hung Byers, A (2011) *Big Data: The next frontier for innovation, competition, and productivity*, McKinsey Global Institute

7 Smolan, R and Erwitt, J (2012) *The Human Face of Big Data*, Sterling, New York

8 Westerman, George, Bonnet, Didier and McAfee, Andrew (2014) The nine elements of digital transformation, *MIT Sloan Management Review*, 7 January

9 Simonson, Itamar and Rosen, Emanuel (2014) *Absolute Value: What really influences customers in the age of (nearly) perfect information*, HarperBusiness

10 See http://www.gfk.com/emoscan/Pages/use-cases.aspx

11 See http://www.bbc.co.uk/news/technology-24803378

12 Kitchin, Rob (2014) *The Data Revolution: Big data, open data, data infrastructures and their consequences*, SAGE Publications Ltd

13 Borgman, C L (2007) *Scholarship in the Digital Age*, MIT Press, Cambridge, MA

14 Kitchin, Rob (2014) (see note 12 above)

15 Golder, Scott A and Macy, Michael W (2014) (see note 4 above)

16 Erickson, T (1999) Persistent conversation: an introduction, *Journal of Computer-Mediated Communication* 4 (4), doi: 10.1111/j.1083-6101.1999.tb00105.x

17 Capgemini (2012) *The deciding factor: Big Data and decision making*, London Economist Intelligence Unit

PART ONE
Current
thinking

Is there a view from nowhere?

02

One of the most prominent claims made by many enthusiasts of big data is that size is everything. In other words, as the sheer volumes of data increase exponentially, alongside the growth in our ability to transfer, store and analyse it, so does our ability to access insights that would not otherwise have been possible by conventional means. Rather than rely on traditional statistical methods of random sampling, it is claimed that we will now be able to make judgements based on all the data, not just a representative portion of it.

As Mayer-Schönberger and Cukier point out,[1] the use of random sampling has long been the backbone of measurement at scale since it reduced the challenges of large-scale data collection to something more manageable. But in an era of big data it is argued that this is becoming a 'second-best' alternative. Why use a sample when you inhabit a world of big data, where instead of having a sample you can have the entire population?

Big data has indeed created many new opportunities for businesses to profit from the knowledge it can deliver. Yet its arrival has also been accompanied by much hyperbole, including the proposition that all this data is somehow objective and of unquestionable reliability. This chapter examines the claims that big data somehow sits beyond traditional limitations of science.

Who are you talking to?

One of the most enduring myths in data collection is that large samples are always more representative. There is the now-infamous example from a poll by *The Literary Digest*[2] published just before the 1936 US presidential election in October 1936. The publication had sent out 10 million postcard questionnaires to prospective voters, of which approximately 2.3 million were returned. The participants were chosen from the magazine's subscription list as well as from automobile registration lists, phone lists and club membership lists.

Interestingly, the magazine had conducted a similar exercise for the previous four presidential elections and successfully predicted the outcome. In this case, however, its declaration that the Republican challenger (Alf Landon) would unseat the incumbent Democrat (Franklin Roosevelt) proved to be a spectacular failure: Roosevelt won by a landslide. The publication folded two years later.

Analysis suggests a number of sources of major errors. Chief among them was the financial environment of the time, with the United States in the midst of the worst depression the country had ever seen. Those on the magazine's (expensive) subscription list, along with those chosen based on car and phone ownership and club membership, would naturally include a larger proportion of some of the better-off members of society who would lean towards the Republican candidate. While in past elections bias based on income differentials had not been such an issue, it was definitely one in the Great Depression.

Another problem was self-selection. Those who took the time to return the postcards very likely had different voting intentions from those that did not bother.

Sources of bias in samples

Of course, researchers have to take bias into account when studying samples and there is a long history of understanding how to ensure that as little occurs as possible. Let's take a brief look at the types of bias that can arise

1 Self-selection bias. This can occur when individuals select themselves into a group, since people who self-select are likely to differ in important ways from the population the researcher wants to analyse. There was obviously an

element of self-selection in those who chose to return the questionnaires to *The Literary Digest*.

2 Under-coverage bias. This can happen when a relevant segment of the population is ignored. Again, *The Literary Digest* poll didn't include less well-off individuals who were more likely to support the Democratic incumbent, Roosevelt, than his opponent.

3 Survivorship bias. This arises from concentrating on the people or things that 'survived' some process and inadvertently overlooking those that did not – such as companies that have failed being excluded from performance studies because they no longer exist.

It's also worth mentioning other sources of bias besides the selection of the sample itself. These might include respondents being reluctant to reveal the truth (surveys of drinking habits is a good example here), a low response rate and/or the wording/order of the questions in a survey.

Diligence can go a long way to overcoming most sampling problems, as Good and Hardin conclude:[3]

> With careful and prolonged planning, we may reduce or eliminate many potential sources of bias, but seldom will we be able to eliminate all of them. Accept bias as inevitable and then endeavour to recognize and report all exceptions that do slip through the cracks.

The upsides of sampling

Clearly a census approach (ie having access to information about the whole population for analysis) is an attractive proposition for researchers. Nevertheless, sampling has continued to dominate for several reasons:

● Handling costs: many brands have huge transaction databases. They will typically skim off about 10 per cent of the records in order to be able to analyse them because otherwise the processing time and costs are just too substantial. Brands want to ensure they have sufficient data to be able to provide adequate representativeness as well as being able to delve into particular demographics or segments.

- Quality: as W Edwards Deming, the statistician whose work was seminal to the quality measurement movement, argued,[4] the quality of a study is often better with sampling than with a census: 'Sampling possesses the possibility of better interviewing (testing), more thorough investigation of missing, wrong or suspicious information, better supervisions and better processing than is possible with complete coverage.' Research findings substantiate this assertion. More than 90 per cent of survey error in one study was from non-sampling error, and 10 per cent from sampling error.[5]

- Speed: sampling often provides relevant information more quickly than much larger data sets as the logistics of collection, handling and analysing larger data sets can be time-consuming.

Bigger samples are not always better

One important issue that market researchers are very familiar with is that as the size of a sample increases, the margin of error decreases. However, it's important to note that this is not open-ended: the amount by which the margin of error decreases, while substantial between sample sizes of 200 and 1500, then tends to level off, as Table 2.1 shows.

So while accuracy does improve with bigger samples, the rate of improvement does fall off rapidly. In addition, every time a sub-sample is selected, the margin of error needs to be recalibrated, which is why market researchers, for example, will often try to work with as large a sample as possible.

Big data and sampling

Big data is often accompanied by an underlying assumption that all records can be obtained, so we are dealing with the total population,

TABLE 2.1 Margin of error as a function of sample size

Sample size	Margin of error
200	±6.9%
400	±4.9%
700	±3.7%
1000	±3.1%
1200	±2.8%
1500	±2.5%
2000	±2.2%
3000	±1.8%
4000	±1.5%
5000	±1.4%

not a sample of that population. According to Mayer-Schönberger and Cukier, having the full data set is beneficial for a number of reasons:

- It not only offers more freedom to explore but also enables researchers to drill down to levels of detail previously undreamt of.

- Because of the way the data is collected it is less tainted by the biases associated with sampling.

- It can also help uncover previously-hidden information since the size of the data set makes it possible to see connections that would not be possible in smaller samples.

They point to the advent of the Google Flu Trends survey. Google uses aggregated search terms to estimate flu activity, to the extent that the analysis can reveal the spread of flu down to the level of a city (there is more about its efficacy in Chapter 6). Another example is the work done by Albert-László Barabási, a leading researcher on the science of network theory. He studied the anonymous logs of mobile phone users from a wireless operator serving almost a fifth of one European country's population over a four-month period. Using the data set of 'everyone', he and his team were able to uncover a variety of insights concerning human behaviours that he claims would probably have been impossible with a smaller sample.[6]

This thinking does indeed suggest that big data is the holy grail for researchers wanting to understand human behaviour. But there are a number of challenges associated with its use, as discussed below.

Big data sampling

This might seem counter-intuitive, but it is generally more practical *not* to be working with total data sets. The educational and policy studies organization, the Aspen Institute, produced a paper[7] in 2010, just as the big data avalanche began to acquire serious momentum, which asked 'Is more actually less?'

The paper quotes Hal Varian, Google Chief Economist, discussing the premise that smaller data sets can never be reliable proxies for big data:

> At Google... the engineers take one-third of a per cent of the daily data as a sample, and calculate all the aggregate statistics off my representative sample... Generally, you'll get just as good a result from the random sample as from looking at everything.

Who are you talking to?

Big data proponents argue that not only does this abundance of data enable you to find things out you didn't know you were looking for, but it can also produce new and useful insights. That is true, as long as you know the right questions to ask to find meaningful answers. Closely aligned to that is the need to ensure that the big data available represents the entire population of interest and that its provenance ensures representativeness and accuracy.

Let's return to the work Barabási carried out with the network operator. Yes, it very possibly represented millions of individuals. But before making general assumptions you would have to know much more about which operator it was in order to understand the context and environment. For instance, does it have a higher proportion of business customers and, if so, was that allowed for? Or are its customers older, or more family-oriented? Only then can you begin to decide what sort of biases would emerge.

Kate Crawford of the MIT Center for Civic Media is not confident that big data is always what it seems:[8]

> Data and data sets are not objective; they are creations of human design. We give numbers their voice, draw inferences from them, and define their meaning through our interpretations. Hidden biases in both the collection and analysis stages present considerable risks, and are as important to the big-data equation as the numbers themselves.

She has studied the examples of error that can accrue from a lack of representativeness in social networks, which are a key source of big data for many researchers. She highlights what she calls the 'signal problem'. During the devastating Hurricane Sandy in the Northeast United States in 2012 there were more than 20 million tweets between 27 October and 1 November. A study combining those with data from the location app Foursquare made expected findings, such as grocery shopping peaking the evening before the storm, and unexpected ones such as nightlife picking up the day after. She notes, however, that a large proportion of the tweets came from Manhattan, which had been less affected by the storm compared to the havoc affecting regions outside the city. The overall picture would thus be misleading since those most affected were suffering power blackouts and lack of cellphone access.

The caveman effect

Another type of bias arises from the fact that the simple act of choosing what data you are going to work with is by its very nature a constraint. You would think that big data should, in principle, avoid the bias inherent in survey questionnaire design. However, what data is *actually* captured and what that data represents is going to make all the difference to the findings.

There is a rich literature detailing what has been called the 'caveman effect'.[9] Much of what we know about our prehistoric ancestors comes from what we have uncovered intact from thousands of years ago in caves, such as paintings from nearly 40,000 years ago, fire pits, middens (dumps for domestic waste) and burial sites. There might well have been other examples of prehistoric life, well beyond cave life, including paintings on trees, animal skins or hillsides, which have long since disappeared. Our ancestors are thus associated with caves because the data still exists, not because they necessarily lived most of their lives in caves.

The data held by mobile network operators is a reflection of this. It is typically what's needed for billing purposes, so will include details of number of call minutes, texts sent and data minutes. It will rarely include other activity such as that via third party sites like Facebook. So while there may be millions of records, they don't always represent all activity and will thus shape the nature of any analysis undertaken.

In addition, there will always be a need to consider which variables to examine. Jesper Andersen, a statistician, computer scientist and co-founder of Freerisk, warns[10] that 'cleaning the data' – or deciding which attributes and variables matter and which can be ignored – is a dicey proposition, because:

> it removes the objectivity from the data itself. It's a very opinionated process of deciding what variables matter. People have this notion that you can have an agnostic method of running over data, but the truth is that the moment you touch the data, you've spoiled it. For any operation, you have destroyed that objective basis for it.

In essence, the 'caveman effect' is the big data equivalent of the survey's questionnaire bias. Size is not everything, nor does it mean we get better cut-through into 'the truth'. It is not an objective process. There are decisions to be made and those decisions will introduce bias. All approaches have bias. It's unavoidable. The challenge is identifying the nature of this bias and then either correcting it or allowing for it in the interpretation of the data.

An example of this is again from Kate Crowford. Data sets, she asserts, are intricately linked to physical place and human culture. When the City of Boston developed an app to help inhabitants identify the worst potholes (which plague the city streets) it found that, unsurprisingly, more alerts came from smartphone owners. However, these are less well-represented among lower-income groups. So the city had to take that into account when allocating resources.

Differences between online and offline worlds

Zeynep Tufekci, a professor at the University of North Carolina and a fellow at Princeton's Center for Information Technology Policy, compared[11] using Twitter to biological testing carried out on fruit flies. These insects are usually chosen for lab work because they are adaptable to the settings, are easy to breed, have rapid and stereotypical life cycles and as adults are small enough to work with.

The parallel she makes is that the research on fruit flies takes place in a laboratory, not in real life. She likens this to using Twitter as the 'model organism' for social media in big data analysis. Since Twitter users make up only about 10 per cent of the US population, some demographic or social groups won't be represented. The result? More data, she argues, does not necessarily mean more insight as it does not necessarily reflect real life.

And this is a fair challenge, as perhaps there are significant differences between the way in which we operate in an online and offline environment. This not only applies to social networking sites but also the way in which we may undertake transactions with online brands. In some ways these are straightforward so, for example, in an online world we have no geographic constraints. From the UK we can communicate with someone in Australia as easily as someone sitting next to us. And there are no temporal limitations so we can wait before responding to an email, status update or marketing message in a way that social convention will not allow us to do so in face-to-face communication. This clearly allows us to be more deliberative about the way in which we then choose to present ourselves.

Anonymity permitted by online transactions is also an important difference so we can create new personas for ourselves and respond in ways that we would not even consider doing face to face, as testified by the level of vitriolic conversations that take place on some social networking sites.

However, whilst studies have tended to focus on the relative richness of offline conversations compared to online, Golder and Macy[12] point out in their review of online versus offline environments that readily available histories of individuals (whether in social history or on a CRM system) and the imaginative use of the media (such as the use of emoji or the Twitter @reply) mean that the medium is perhaps richer than we had given it credit for.

There are of course concerns about the value of generalizing from the online to the offline populations. The online population is typically younger, better educated and more affluent than the overall population. There is also biased representation in online environments, so although some segments of the population might have access, the breadth and depth of their involvement is very different to that of the general online population.

We can also argue that any form of research has its challenges in terms of representativeness. Within market research much is now done via online surveys with a representative sample of the population that have chosen to be members of research panels. Whilst the representativeness of these panels is good enough for most purposes (and to justify the significantly reduced costs) it is still nevertheless not necessarily the gold standard. Governments are more likely to pay for probability-based sampling, which is the closest you get to a fully representative sample (excluding census surveys), but even here we have to take into account the proportion of the population that refuse to participate. And academics who run experiments have also had questions raised concerning the representativeness of their research participants, who Henrich *et al*[13] dubbed as WEIRD – an acronym for Western, educated, industrialized, rich and democratic.

Each research approach has its own upsides and challenges. As Golder and Macy point out, even though the online world is not identical to the offline one, it is still real. People who want status, social approval and attention will bring these same motivations to their online activity. We still have to navigate the same social obstacles online as well as offline when dealing with brands, seeking information, pursuing friendship or romance. And as we saw in Chapter 1, as the world is becoming increasingly datafied, our ability to capture what was once offline and therefore off limits is rapidly growing.

Concluding thoughts

The message from this chapter is that total objectivity can, at times, be illusory. There are always trade-offs to be made when conducting research. It is less about collecting data that has no bias but understanding which biases you are willing to accept in the data. Of course some biases will not be pertinent to the question you are trying to explore and others may have a minimal effect, but correcting them is too costly and time-consuming to be worth the investment. It's worth considering that sampling is an art and science that has been brilliantly perfected over many years to mitigate against the effects of bias. As we start seeing that big data is not an *n*=all paradigm (where the entire population is covered), it may be no bad thing for big data analytics to start considering how best to apply sampling in this very different context. Unfortunately, much of the time these issues are simply not properly considered and as such analysis is done which is then quickly discredited. The lesson here is to know your territory, mitigate against bias where you can but understand it where you cannot.

Notes

1 Mayer-Schönberger, Viktor and Cukier, Kenneth (2012) *Big Data: a revolution that will transform how we live, work and think*, John Murray

2 More information about the *Literary Digest* poll can be found at http://www.math.uah.edu/stat/data/LiteraryDigest.html

3 Good, Phillip I and Hardin, James W (2012) *Common Errors in Statistics (and how to avoid them)*, 4th ed, Wiley

4 Deming, W Edwards (1960) *Sample Design in Business Research*, 1st ed, Wiley Classics Library

5 Cooper, Donald R and Emory, C William (1995) *Business Research Methods*, 5th ed, Richard D. Irwin

6 http://online.wsj.com/articles/SB10001424052748704547604576263261679848814

7 Bollier, David (2010) *The promise and peril of big data*, The Aspen Institute

8 Crawford, Kate (2013) The Hidden Biases in Big Data, *Harvard Business Review*, HBR Blog Network, 1 April

9 http://en.wikipedia.org/wiki/Sampling_bias

10 In Bollier, David (2010) (See note 7 above)

11 Tufekci, Zeynep (2013) Big Data: pitfalls, methods and concepts for an emergent field [online] http://ssrn.com/abstract=2229952

12 Golder, Scott A and Macy, Michael W (2014) Digital footprints: opportunities and challenges for online social research, *Annual Review of Sociology* 40, pp 129–52

13 Henrich J, Heine, S J and Norenzayan, A (2010) The weirdest people in the world? *Behavioural and Brain Sciences* 33, pp 61–83

Choose your weapons

03

Organizations have always measured things. Measures can tell businesses where they have come from, where they are now and where they might be going. They provide the ability to keep score, to warn of potential dangers and help scout out new opportunities.

It would therefore seem logical to herald the era of big data as offering even more chances to get measurement right. However, having too much data is perhaps becoming almost as much of a problem as having too little: it can be tempting to select data to focus on because we can rather than because it is 'right'.

The result is that we are in danger of assuming that having swathes of data to analyse will lead to findings that are grounded in reality. It's what the late Nobel Prize-winning physicist Richard Feynman called the 'cargo cult' theory,[1] or the illusion that something is scientific when it has no basis in fact. He described how in World War II, a group of islanders in the South Seas watched the US military busily build and maintain airstrips on their islands as bases from which to defend against Japanese attacks following Pearl Harbor.

After the war, and the departure of the Americans, the islanders wanted to continue to enjoy all the material benefits the airplanes had brought: the 'cargo from the skies'. So they reportedly built replica runways, a wooden hut and wooden headset for their version of a controller and carried out religious rituals in the hope that it would all return. But, of course, the airplanes never came, even though the islanders went about it 'scientifically'. In other words, the data they used as an input was flawed.

It is certainly true that companies today have a big advantage over their predecessors: no matter how lean they are, they have access to a wealth of data that wouldn't have been available just a few years ago. But just because this data is available, there is little guidance on:

- which metric to track;
- what you need to be measuring;
- what the landscape looks like;
- where to start;
- how to order your thinking.

The actual task of selecting your metrics is thus anything but straightforward. Choose the wrong one and you can change people's behaviour in the wrong way, with unintended consequences.

The perils of vanity metrics

By ignoring the reasons why we collect these statistics, misunderstanding the context, or not figuring out what questions we want answered, metrics can often prove meaningless. This propensity to measure the wrong things has become even more of an issue with the advent of web analytics, with its avalanche of data from online activity. Organizations are now struggling to know which measures of the vast array they have at their disposal they should be focusing on.

As Alistair Croll and Benjamin Yoskovitz point out in their book *Lean Analytics*,[2] it's far too easy to fall in love with what they call 'vanity' metrics. These are the ones that consistently move up and make us feel good but really don't help us make decisions that affect actual performance.

Croll and Yoskovitz list eight of what they see as the worst offenders:

- Number of hits: from the early, 'foolish' days of the web, it's pretty meaningless. Count people instead.

- Number of page views: again, unless the business model is based on page views, count people.

- Number of visits: how do you know if this is one person who visits a number of times, or many people visiting once?

- Number of unique visitors: this doesn't really tell you anything about why they visited, why they stayed or why they left.

- Number of followers/friends/likes: unless you can get them to do something useful, it's just a popularity contest.

- Time on site/number of pages: a poor substitute for actual engagement or activity unless it is relevant for the business. It could tell you something, however, if the time spent is on the complaints/support pages.

- Emails collected: the number might look good, but again, it doesn't tell you much that's really useful.

- Number of downloads: this can boost your position in the app store rankings, but by themselves the numbers create little of real value.

Of course, we don't intentionally select the wrong metrics. We assume they are the right ones. However, as marketer Seth Godin points out, this is dangerous: 'When we fall in love with a proxy, we spend our time improving the proxy instead of focusing on our original (more important) goal.'[3]

Eric Ries, author of *The Lean Startup*,[4] considers that vanity metrics fail what he calls the 'so what?' test. He favours solid metrics that actually help improve the business, such as revenue, sales volume, customer retention and those that show a traceable pattern whereby the actions of existing customers can create new ones. Knowing how many registered members or Facebook friends you have won't have much impact. But metrics that give invaluable information such as monitoring loyal customers so that you can engage with them will actually grow the business.

As the next section discusses, the first step is to choose what questions you want to ask. Only then can an organization determine the right measures to apply.

Thinking about thinking: defining the questions

Perhaps the biggest challenge that brands face is venturing into the unknown and finding it difficult to plan for what they don't know. The first step, therefore, actually needs to be a step back to consider where you want to go.

Search online and there is no end of helpful advice and much that can be learned from the experience of others in choosing what to measure and why. However, while this can provide useful guidance, every situation is different and every brand has its own particular challenges. But, even more importantly, every brand should differentiate itself and as such needs its own metrics to be driving the business.

You have to start with the direction in mind before knowing what questions you want metrics to answer. For businesses, this calls for a continual reframing of the questions that need to be asked, and the measures that need to be collected, in order to keep abreast of constantly changing markets and technology. The box below gives some examples of how very different frames can lead to very different answers.

A question of framing

Research[5] reveals how framing affects many different realms of decision-making. Our minds react to the way in which a question is asked or information presented. So, for example:

- a '95 per cent effective' condom appears more effective than one with a '5 per cent failure rate';

- people prefer to take a 5 per cent raise when inflation is 12 per cent than take a 7 per cent cut when inflation is zero;

- considering two packages of ground beef, most people would pick the one labelled, '80 per cent lean' over the one labelled, '20 per cent fat'.

The researcher Elizabeth Loftus has demonstrated how, after watching the same video of a car crash, those people who are asked, 'How fast were the cars going when they contacted?' recalled slower speeds in comparison to those that were asked, 'How fast was the car going when they crashed?'

Framing is inevitable. An issue has to be presented somehow, a question has to be asked; there is no such thing as a totally objective view of the world. The challenge is to spot the frame that is being used. In poker there is a saying that if you can't spot the sucker, it's you. Awareness is the start of regaining control. We can then choose whether to accept or reject the frame that has been presented to us and consider whether there are alternative frames we would prefer to use.

Possibly the most important thing to bear in mind is that the measures you choose are not viewed as an adjunct stuck down in the digital department but an integral part of the business. The challenge is to choose the right metrics to pull the data provided into a useable form, to report the findings, and to have your organization coalesce around them.

Donald Marchand and Joe Peppard,[6] writing in the *Harvard Business Review*, believe this needs an understanding of how people create and use information. They studied more than 50 international companies in a variety of industries to identify optimal ways for companies to 'frame' the way they approach data. They argue that a big data or analytics project simply cannot be treated like a conventional large IT project because the IT project is by its very nature limited to answering questions already asked.

Instead, such a project should focus on the exploration of information by framing questions to which the data *might* provide answers, develop hypotheses and then conduct iterative experiments to gain knowledge and understanding. Along with IT professionals, therefore, teams should also include specialists in the cognitive and behavioural sciences who understand how people perceive problems, use information and analyse data in developing solutions, ideas and knowledge. Analytical techniques and controlled experiments are tools for thinking, but it is people who do the actual thinking and learning.

Frameworks to help select metrics

There are a number of frameworks available to help with this process of identifying what the appropriate metrics should be that will help an organization meet its particular goals. In this section we review a number of them. This is by no means prescriptive. Instead, it is used more to illustrate how important it is to spend time 'thinking about thinking' before plunging in and selecting metrics, which, if they don't reflect your own priorities and challenges, can have long-term, unexpected consequences.

The Donald Rumsfeld model

> ... there are known knowns; there are things we know that we know. There are known unknowns; that is to say, there are things that we now know we don't know. But there are also unknown unknowns – there are things we do not know we don't know.

The former US Secretary of Defense, Donald Rumsfeld, famously made his comment at a press briefing in 2002, where he addressed the absence of evidence linking the government of Iraq with the supply of weapons of mass destruction to terrorist groups.

His somewhat unusual phrasing got huge coverage, to the extent that he used it as the title of his subsequent autobiography, *Known and Unknown: A memoir*.[7] Opinions were divided about his comments. For instance, it earned him the 2003 Foot in Mouth Award and was criticized as an abuse of language by, among others, the Plain English Campaign. However, he had his defenders – among them, Canadian columnist Mark Steyn, who called it 'in fact a brilliant distillation of quite a complex matter'.[8]

Croll and Yoskovitz[9] made good use of Rumsfeld's phrase to design a way of thinking about metrics, in their book *Lean Analytics: Use data to build a better startup faster*. Although their focus is obviously startups, the same principles can apply to any organization.

Their view is that analytics have a role to play in all four of Rumsfeld's quadrants:

- Things we know we know (facts). Metrics which check our assumptions – such as open rates or conversion rates. It's easy to believe in conventional wisdom that 'we always close 50 per cent of sales', for example. Having hard metrics tests the things we think 'we know we know'.

- Things we know we don't know (questions). Where we know we need information to fill gaps in our understanding.

- Things we don't know we know (intuition). Here the use of metrics can test our intuitions, turning hypotheses into evidence.

- Things we don't know we don't know (exploration). Analytics can help us find the nugget of opportunity on which to build a business.

While some of the rationale behind these may feel a little strangulated in order to fit an elegant framework, there is nevertheless something quite appealing about this approach, not least because of the way it engages an audience to think about what is known and not known.

It also introduces the concept of exploratory versus reporting metrics, an important distinction to make but one which is often confused. Reporting metrics support the business to optimize its operation to meet the strategy while exploratory metrics set out to find, as the authors say, the nugget of opportunity. These 'unknown unknowns' are where the magic lies. They might lead down plenty of wrong paths, but hopefully towards some moment of brilliance that creates value for the business (see box below for more discussion about data exploration).

The data lab

To get the best out of big data organizations have to do two things well, argue Thomas Redman and Bill Sweeney.[10]

First, they have to find interesting, novel and useful insights about the real world in data. Then they have to turn those insights into products and services. Each of those demands a separate department.

The first is the data equivalent of a scientific laboratory, peopled with talented, diverse teams of data scientists with license to explore in whichever directions their hypotheses take them but within a well-managed framework.

The second, the data factory, is where process engineers and others with technical skills take the most promising insights from the lab and attempt to translate them into products and services. Each should have different time scales and different metrics.

Nevertheless, in any kind of business, both types of metric are essential. In smaller startups the balance will often be more tilted towards the 'things we don't know' while in more established businesses there may be more focus on measuring the 'things we know'. But any business ignores either side of this at their peril.

The Gregor model

Moving more in the direction of thinking about the way in which to consider 'information systems', Shirley Gregor,[11] professor of information systems at the Australian National University in Canberra, Australia, identified a taxonomy of 'theories' or different types of knowledge. It makes good sense to use this in thinking about different categories of metrics. The beauty of this approach is that it emphasizes that we don't always need metrics to have a direct relationship with business success. Sometimes it is just as important (if not more so at times) to look at metrics that help us to understand the landscape, for example. The relationship with outcomes is still there but less immediately obvious and more indirect.

The categories Gregor identifies are shown in Table 3.1.

Analysis

This really sets out to describe what the landscape looks like. So, for example, we need to know what the size of an addressable market is: what exactly is the scale of opportunity for our business and how

TABLE 3.1 Taxonomy of theory types

Theory Type	Attributes
Analysis	Says what it is
Explanation	Says what it is, how, why, when and where
Prediction	Says what it is and what will be
Explanation and prediction	Says what is, how, why, when, where and what will be
Design and action	Says how to do something

SOURCE Adapted from Gregor, S (2006) The nature of theory in information systems, *MIS Quarterly* **30** (3), pp 611–42

does this vary by customer group? A customer segmentation may fall into this category, identifying different clusters of consumers in a way that meets the needs of our business.

Explanation

This theory type could be called a theory for understanding, as it has an emphasis on showing how we can understand the world, to bring about a new understanding. Much market research could arguably fall into this category, giving us insight into why people are behaving in particular ways.

Prediction

This is prediction with understanding and as such goes to the heart of much of the discussion in this book. However, it is important to acknowledge that at times we do not always need causality. As Gregor points out, reasons to justify the attribution of causality might not yet have been uncovered. She points out that Captain Cook theorized well that regular intakes of lemons prevented scurvy, even though he did not know exactly why.

Explanation and prediction

This is in a sense the 'gold standard' for a metric. Not only can we understand the mechanism underlying a phenomenon, ie we can explain why something moves, but we can also predict the nature of that movement. So, for example, we may consider a theory or approach relating to customer satisfaction that appears to make sense for our particular business. We can develop metrics that measure different elements of the approach and then measure the degree to which these are able to predict particular outcomes such as customer retention or customer value. So we not only have something that predicts outcomes but we understand the principles underneath this.

Design and action

This type of theory says how to do something and is reflected in the huge area of design thinking. Typical examples of areas that may need to be measured here are: capturing the common mistakes that people make; the length of time it takes someone to get to the checkout; the speed at which drivers are using a particular road, and so on. If we measure how people are doing certain activities we can start seeking to improve them based on our principles of what makes for a successful business.

Of course there is plenty of overlap and inter-relationship between these different categories, which is inevitable. There is no particular hierarchy, although of course a premium is always placed on prediction. However, each of these arguably has a place and should be considered as part of the measurement regime for any brand.

The data type vs business objective model

A contrasting and very pragmatic approach is offered by Salvatore Parise and Bala Iyer, professors in the Technology, Operations, and Information Management division at Babson College, and Dan Vesset, programme vice president of IDC's business analytics research.[12] They have made the distinction between business objective (measurement and experimentation) and type of data (transactional versus non-transactional), as shown in Figure 3.1 below.

The four different categories are summarized as follows:

- Performance management: The data used here is typically structured and accessed from internal systems such as CRM systems. This is the type of analysis that can be used for dashboard input for the effective management of the business.

- Data exploration: This type of analysis is exploring the transactional data in ways that might not have been considered previously. It often uses predictive modelling techniques although this should be one of a range of interesting paths through to effectively mining the data.

- Social analytics: This is ongoing measurement of the brand in social media, establishing the brand's ongoing performance on metrics such as awareness, engagement and reach.

- Decision science: Involves conducting experiments and analytics of non-transactional data. So this may include web scraping tools to collect data from social media that is then used for test and sentiment analysis.

The creation of these four separate categories allows us to think more carefully about the nature of the relationship between the business objective and the available data. A side benefit is that it also encourages us to consider how the same data can be used in different ways, so that while

FIGURE 3.1 Big data framework

		Measurement	Experimentation
DATA TYPE	**Transactional**	Social analytics	Decision science
	Non-transactional	Performance management	Data exploration

BUSINESS OBJECTIVE

SOURCE Adapted from Parise Salvatore and Iyer, Bala (2012) Four strategies to capture and create value from big data, *Ivey Business Journal*, July/August social media data may often be used by many companies as a performance metric, it can also be used to identify new issues and opportunities for the brand.

What this discussion highlights is that while 'thinking about thinking' may seem a little abstract at times, particularly in the day-to-day business of organizational life, the danger of not having a clear structure for thinking can result in a very unfocused set of activities. This affects not only the data analysts trying to make some kind of sense of the ever-increasing waves of data entering the organization but also those involved in setting and executing strategy within the business.

There are no definitive ways to do this. However, any of the approaches listed above are a good place to start and indeed there are undoubtedly other examples from the literature. It may also be useful to construct your own framework depending on your own priorities and challenges. If there is a lack of clarity about the different purposes to which analytics are being put in an organization then this will emerge during the exercise.

Tracking your metrics

The discussion of which metrics to pick must include a reference to the way in which they are adopted by the organization, largely in the form of scorecards and dashboards. These are typically those metrics that measure and guide the performance of the organization – the factory rather than the laboratory – although the boundaries can be fluid when necessary.

Balanced scorecards and dashboards

The balanced scorecard was originally developed over twenty years ago by Kaplan and Norton[13] with the aim of the giving organizations a more rounded picture of their performance by including non-financial measures that encompassed customers, innovation and quality issues. It covered a much wider spectrum than businesses had done before and has evolved into a performance measurement and management tool designed to clarify strategy, monitor progress and define and manage action plans.

In Kaplan and Norton's view, an organization should be assessed from four perspectives:

- Learning and growth: encouraging a culture of learning in terms of both individual and corporate self-improvement.

- Customers: appreciating that customer satisfaction and retention is the source of growth.

- Internal business processes: aligning internal processes with customer requirements.

- Financial: providing a detailed and comprehensive picture of the financial performance.

There are two main reasons why the balanced scorecard seemed to fall in popularity over the last few years. First, it wasn't always applied in the right strategic manner. Executives would instead turn it into the equivalent of a tactical 'dashboard' reflecting short-term results (see box below for a discussion of the difference between dashboards and scorecards). At the same time, it became fashionable to focus on having a smaller number of metrics to act as lode stars for the organization, such as the net promoter score for customer loyalty.

The scorecard is now experiencing somewhat of a resurgence in popularity, with the overwhelming increase in data coming into organizations provoking interest in finding ways to monitor, organize and exploit it effectively.

Configured and populated with the right information, balanced scorecards help ensure that organizations keep on course as measured by key performance indicators. The need for this type of guidance is more important than ever now given the mass of analytics streaming in from all corners of the organization.

The use of dashboards and balanced scorecards does run the danger of sounding very 'corporate' and has gained something of a reputation as being out of step with the need to be nimble and agile. Nevertheless, any business, even a startup, still has to choose the

The difference between scorecards and dashboards

What's the difference between scorecards and dashboards? Gary Cokins, author of the CGMA book *Strategic Business Management: From planning to performance*, offers guidelines to help distinguish between dashboards and scorecards.[14]

Scorecards monitor the progress towards accomplishing strategic objectives. A scorecard offers regular snapshots of performance associated with an organization's strategic objective and plans. He describes two main characteristics of scorecards. First, each key performance indicator (KPI) has to have a predefined target measure. Secondly, these strategic KPIs should include project-based measures such as milestones, progress towards completion and degree of planned vs accomplished outcomes, as well as metrics such as customer satisfaction and delivery.

Dashboards monitor and measure processes and outputs. A dashboard is operational and reports information typically more frequently than scorecards. Like a car's dashboard, which lets drivers check their current speed, fuel level and engine temperature at a glance, they offer more real-time metrics but say little about the overall direction.

right metrics to track their performance of, even while exploring new territory.

Dave McClure, a San Francisco-based venture capitalist and entrepreneur who founded and runs the business incubator 500 Startups, believes that despite a startup's size the fundamental principles still apply. He has drawn up a list[15] of the most useful measures for businesses. While it is aimed at startups, its pragmatic approach will resonate with businesses of all sizes:

- acquisition: find new users;
- activation: get users to try your product;
- retention: make sure those users stick around;
- referral: have your loyal users invite others;
- revenue: hopefully you get to make some money from all this.

From good data to good decisions

Lots of metrics thus don't necessarily lead to good decisions. On the one hand we have tales of Amazon famously using the click-stream and historical purchase data it collects from its 152 million customer accounts to optimize sales through customized results and web pages. In fact, Amazon now holds so much data on its customers and what they buy that it successfully sells the information to brands for product advertising. Data appears to be used well here to make intelligent decisions that support the business.

Understandably, it is less often that we have case studies from companies detailing how they have not made sensible decisions from their data assets. But then there is the tale of the passenger who flew on a major airline business class flight from Portugal to London.[16] The cabin staff told her that they were short of meals and that as she had the fewest loyalty points of all the passengers, they didn't have a lunch for her. Clearly this was the logical reality of a data-driven decision, but one that failed to take into account the context, which was that she was six months pregnant. A fellow passenger donating his meal resolved the issue but did little for the brand relationship.

Decisions based on purely data-driven findings can fail to help us understand the real world and apply common sense. In these instances, such as in the airline example above, it's very easy to miss the intended effect quite significantly.

Psychologist Barry Schwartz talks about this[17] when he refers to 'practical wisdom': the way in which we use our humanity to judge what best to do in a situation. He uses the example of hospital janitors who, despite their job descriptions saying nothing about interactions with other people, often demonstrate great sensitivity to patients in the way they work despite admonitions from their supervisors. Schwartz suggests a wise person is like a jazz musician, who is 'using the notes on the page but dancing around them, inventing combinations that are appropriate for the situation and the people at hand'.

What really matters is the use that's being made of a particular metric and to what end. Data-driven decisions need to take the real world into account, a world that is often ambiguous and ill-defined, with a context that will frequently change. It is also a tall order for any computer to be able to capture the subtlety and personalization that real human beings demonstrate across social contexts. The message is that any measure can be 'the wrong measure' in the wrong hands. And even the 'right' metrics may get a bad name for themselves if they are used in a sloppy or unthinking way as a proxy for something they don't measure very well.

Concluding thoughts

The fact that most organizations, large and small, are now awash with data is no bad thing. In fact it is a huge opportunity for businesses to acquire insight and understanding in ways never before considered possible. However, what is a problem is that most organizations don't step back to consider how the data should be explored and understood. Analysis designed to uncover new insights is confounded with those used to measure performance. There is a lack of attention to which metrics actually make a difference to the business – there is still too much focus on measurement as a function of ease for accessing the number rather than relevance to business outcomes.

There is at times a squeamishness about 'thinking about thinking' but this is what urgently needs to happen for many businesses if they are to organize their data assets in a way that helps drive the business rather than hinder them by a lack of understanding of what they mean and what they are for.

Increasingly much of the challenge for successful businesses is understanding which are the right questions to ask. If we ask different questions from our data than the competition then we are in a better place. There is, however, a danger that questions are framed in a way that is a function of received wisdom rather than from a challenging perspective. Behavioural science is therefore starting to demonstrate how it can have a valuable role to play in assisting with the way we structure our thinking and frame our questions to drive more thoughtful analytics that help drive success through effective differentiation.

But we also need to keep to the front of our minds one of the recurring themes of this book, which is that data does not speak for itself. And this applies to the metrics that we choose. Too often there are examples of individuals absolving responsibility for decision-making in the face of business metrics, forgetting about the fact that the metrics are not ends in themselves.

Notes

1 Feynman, Richard (1997) *Surely You're Joking, Mr. Feynman!* W.W. Norton & Co

2 Croll, Alistair and Yoskovitz, Benjamin (2013) *Lean Analytics: Use data to build a better startup faster*, O'Reilly Media

3 Godin, Seth (2012) Avoiding the False Proxy Trap [online] http://sethgodin.typepad.com/seths_blog/2012/11/avoiding-the-false-proxy-trap.html

4 Ries, Eric (2011) *The Lean Startup: How constant innovation creates radically successful businesses*, Portfolio Penguin

5 Shpancer, Noam (2010) Framing: Your most important and least recognized daily mental activity, *Psychology Today* [online] https://www.psychologytoday.com/blog/insight-therapy/201012/framing-your-most-important-and-least-recognized-daily-ment

6 Marchand, Donald and Peppard, Joe (2013) Why IT fumbles analytics, *Harvard Business Review*, January

7 Rumsfeld, Donald (2012) *Known and Unknown: A memoir*, Sentinel

8 Steyn, Mark (2003) Rummy speaks the truth, not gobbledygook, *Daily Telegraph*, 9 December

9 Croll, Alistair and Yoskovitz, Benjamin (2013) (see note 2 above)

10 Redman, Thomas C and Sweeney, Bill (2013) To Work with Data, You Need a Lab and a Factory, *Harvard Business Review*, 24 April

11 Gregor, S (2006) The nature of theory in information systems, *MIS Quarterly* 30 (3), pp 611–42

12 Parise, Salvatore, Iyer, Bala and Vessel, Dan (2012) Four strategies to capture and create value from big data, *Ivey Business Journal* [online] http://iveybusinessjournal.com/topics/strategy/four-strategies-to-capture-and-create-value-from-big-data#.UpHiKtLQD9U

13 Kaplan, Robert and Norton, David (1996) *The Balanced Scorecard*, Harvard Business School Press

14 See Cokin's 2013 article, The balanced scorecard, strategy maps and dashboards: why are they different? on the CGMA website at http://www.cgma.org/magazine/features/pages/20138186.aspx

15 McClure, David (2007) Startup metrics for pirates [online] http://www.slideshare.net/dmc500hats/startup-metrics-for-pirates-long-version

16 Armstrong, Christine (2013) Polemic: why I worry about data, *Jericho Chambers*, 28 June [online] http://www.jerichochambers.com/polemic-why-i-worry-about-data/

17 Schwartz, Barry (2010) *Practical Wisdom: The right way to do the right thing*, Riverhead Books

Perils and pitfalls

04

As Mark Twain said, 'What gets us into trouble is not what we don't know. It's what we know for sure that just ain't so.' In other words, a person who doesn't know something is cautious, while someone who incorrectly believes that they know something could be making a big mistake. As we saw in the last chapter, it's easy to kid ourselves that we 'know' something when, in fact, we are dealing in spurious 'facts'.

This is probably worth considering in this era of rapid data growth. We tend to place so much weight on the value of data that we are eager to believe in it and act on it, when all the time we might be making serious errors. This is not an inconsequential matter. Brands' strategies, including significant investment decisions, are built on data. Indeed, increasingly we are being encouraged to make data the backbone of functions previously more reliant on human input such as customer service strategies, product development and marketing/sales. So getting it wrong can have severe consequences. To paraphrase Charles Darwin, while false theories do relatively little harm, false facts can seriously retard progress.

This same point has been made by the big data poster child, Nate Silver, who has pointed out that:[1]

We face danger whenever information growth outpaces our understanding of how to process it. The last forty years of human history imply that it can still take a long time to translate information into useful knowledge and that, if we are not careful, we may take a step back in the meantime.

Dangers of reading data: the pitfalls of correlations

So where do the dangers lurk? One of the principle problems is the over-reliance on correlations (the backbone of most predictive models). In a positive correlation the pattern of data of one variable is dependent on the pattern of the data from another variable. So there is a positive correlation between cold weather and home energy usage but a negative correlation between warm weather and the purchase of winter coats.

Whilst every school child will learn about correlation, their education will probably stop at the point that some correlations are statistically significant. That is, it is estimated that the likelihood of that particular pattern occurring by chance is of a sufficiently low probability that we denote it a level of significance. However, it has long been recognized by those working with data that, given a large enough sample size, most data points will have statistically significant correlations, because at some level everything is related to everything else. The danger is that this leads us to believe there are real relationships in the data where in fact the linkage is trivial. The psychologist Paul Meehl famously called this the 'crud factor',[2] or the phenomenon that leads us to believe that there are real relationships in the data where there aren't any. He cites the case of a professor who spent much of 1967 flipping a coin about 300,000 times and finding 50.2 per cent heads, which he calculated to be statistically significant. A clear case where statistical value does not reflect real relationships.

Nate Silver[3] makes the same point as Meehl when he warns that the number of 'meaningful relationships' is not increasing in step with the meteoric increase in amount of data available. We simply generate a larger number of false positives, that is findings that have statistically significant findings but which are manifestly wrong. This is an issue so endemic in data analytics that it led researcher John Ioannidis to suggest that two-thirds of the findings in medical journals were in fact not robust.[4]

Silver argues that our predictions may be even more prone to failure in the era of big data. Since there is an exponential increase in the amount of available information, there is also an accompanying increase in the number of hypotheses to investigate, with a commensurate increase in the number of false positives.

There are of course techniques that can be used to make more sensible use of correlations such as using ranges rather than directional predictions, establishing multiple corroboration and comparing models (Meehl's paper goes into these and others in some detail). But in addition we need something that is used often in market research – contextual expertise. A deep understanding of consumer behaviour and category expertise is often the litmus test to determine whether a statistically significant result has any real validity. But this has an element of human interpretation, which is also not without its challenges.

Dangers of reading data: the frailties of human judgement

If we cannot always rely on statistical techniques to cut through swathes of data to find meaningful patterns then where do we turn? Naturally, we look to ourselves. However, when we acknowledge that human judgement is involved in the analysis of data, we also need to acknowledge the frailties of our judgement. As behavioural economics has taught us, no individual is immune from misinterpreting data. Perhaps this is implicit in the discussion about the qualities of good data scientists: being 'informed sceptics'[5] who balance judgement with analysis and incorporate the key qualities of a sense of wonder, a quantitative knack, persistence and technical skills.[6]

One cognitive function that is critical for any data scientist is the ability to find order and spot patterns in data. As humans we are excellent at doing this, for good evolutionary reasons. These abilities drive new findings and thus our advancement. But as with all cognitive functions, our strength can also be a weakness if, for instance, we see patterns when in fact none exist.

As Thomas Gilovich points out in his classic book *How We Know What isn't So: The fallibility of human reason in everyday life,*[7] one of the problems we encounter when looking at data is that it's very hard for us to see when it is random and when, in fact, there are patterns. When looking at a truly random sequence we tend to think there are patterns in the data because it somehow looks too ordered or 'lumpy'.[8] For example, as Gilovich points out, when we throw a coin twenty times there is a 50 per cent chance of getting four heads in a row, a 25 per cent chance of five in a row, and a 10 per cent chance of a run of six. But if you give this sequence to most individuals they will consider that these are patterns in the data and not at all random. This explains the 'hot hand' fallacy in which we think we are on a winning streak in whatever it may be – from cards to basketball to football. In each of these areas where the data is random but happens to include a sequence, we massively over-interpret the importance of this pattern.

This effect does not only apply to numeric data, but also to analysis of visuals. This is particularly important in the context of this book as visualization is rapidly becoming a key element of big data analytics. A good illustration of 'fallacy patterns' occurred in the latter part of World War II, when the Germans launched a particularly intense bombing campaign on London. It was a commonly held view at the time that the bombs were landing in clusters, which made some parts of London more dangerous than others.[9] However, after the war, analysis of the data showed that the bombs had in fact landed in a random sequence and no part of London had been more dangerous than another.

The pitfalls of storytelling

Allied to our desire to find patterns is the tendency to want to create stories as a way of making sense of the world and creating order and meaning. The problem is that a story represents a particular interpretation of events (ie data) and of course, is rarely told in a consistent way.

This is nicely illustrated by the classic 'choice blindness' experiment,[10] which showed participants two pictures of different people of the opposite sex: the participant had to choose which they considered more attractive. The experimenter then took the photos away and showed them their 'choice' a minute or two later, asking them to explain their selection. Little did the participant know that the experimenter had switched the photos and they were now busy explaining their choice but for the wrong photo, completely oblivious to the fact they were finding a story to fit the photo they had rejected. This highlights the dangers of the way in which we can be oblivious to the determinants of our decisions, busily post-rationalizing a possibly arbitrary choice.

So while we are born storytellers, and we want a narrative, the recipient of any story should realize that this is an interpretation of the data and should remain open to other perspectives. Who is the storyteller and, as we asked in the previous chapter, how are they framing the issue? Are there implicit assumptions running through it that we should be questioning? What have they decided is relevant and what is irrelevant? Surely a reader needs to understand the author's view of the world and their personal philosophy to appreciate the nature of the frame that will inevitably be applied. Some of the risks of story-telling are highlighted below:

- We have a tendency to prefer particular types of story. So, for example, because we dislike uncertainty we will seek out stories that we can easily comprehend. We will therefore be attracted to stories that reference a framework of thinking we are familiar with even when more complex interpretations have greater explanatory value.

- The more readily something is brought to mind the more likely it is to influence us. So we worry more about dying in a plane crash than a car accident, despite the odds, simply because plane accidents are reported more often. We are all aware of the power of an anecdote from personal experience or the recounting of a tale from a market research focus group. So, again, more colourful stories can win out at the expense of the more worthy but possibly more valid tale.

- In the process of simply listening to the story we are being primed to see the world in a different way. So, to give a simplistic example, a person who sees the word 'yellow' will recognize the word 'banana' more quickly. The lasting legacy of a tale being told well is that we can then tend to only seek out information that is consistent with the story. This 'confirmation bias' means that we seek out data that confirms, rather than tests, our interpretation. And when we get new information we tend to interpret it in a way that is self-serving. So we will often 'fix' our stories alarmingly quickly.

And storytelling also has a potentially more damaging side effect, one that is very much part of the theme for this book. It starts to obfuscate our relationship with causality, as discussed below.

Mixing up narrative and causality

According to Nassim Taleb, author of the brilliant book *Black Swan*,[11] we try to make sense of all the data around us because there are costs attached to information storage. So the more orderly we can make that information then the easier and less costly it is to store in our minds. This means that we prefer our data to be more ordered and less random, so we have a drive to reduce the number of dimensions that we handle and therefore place complex data into a much simpler order. Taleb considers that this is not only the purpose of narrative but also causality. We will try to attribute causality to events so that we can explain and understand, rather than leaving us to deal with the complexity and randomness of the world. And the purpose of imposing a narrative is that it can generate a sense of chronology, so both move in a single direction. The narrative means that we tend then to recall those facts that fit the story, that meet the requirements of the causality the narrative has perpetuated. We then don't recall the true sequence of events but a reconstructed one that makes the causality appear much more straightforward than it was.

But our tendency is not to think of ourselves operating in this way. We tend to think that we are much more objective and rational beings. So a very powerful metaphor is that of the brain as a computer or rather a flawed version of our silicon brethren. This is vigorously promoted by 'The Singularity',[12] a movement that has been highly successful in establishing a model that posits technology will ultimately have far greater intelligence than humans, thus rendering our capabilities redundant. The movement is headed by Ray Kurzweil and has a 'University' based in California which is backed by many of the world's leading technology companies.

This idea has been accepted to an astonishing degree, not only in business circles but also in mainstream media and our culture generally. And whilst 'The Singularity' between humans and machines is not due to arrive until 2045, the 'computer as an enhanced brain' is already an important and influential metaphor that is shaping the way we see the world and our expectations of what technology can deliver.

Perhaps this does not sound all that surprising because we have got so used to the idea that technology is a reflection of ourselves. The trouble is that it is very easy to get caught up in a metaphor, assuming this reflects reality, particularly when it is implicit and not overt and stated. So why does this matter? It matters because the metaphor of the brain as an outboard computer is driving the notion around big data that all we need is technological know-how in order to understand human behaviour. It encourages us to believe that the stories we tell ourselves from scanning the data are reality and we are less likely to consider alternative, more complex explanations.

The consequences of this are significant. The biggest organizational risk is that belief in a particular narrative can slow a company down, fixing its way of seeing the world instead of having a more agile approach that recognizes the complexity of the markets in which it operates. A traditional 'predict and control' strategy is then followed, based on a more rigid way of seeing the world rather than a more nimble 'measure and react' approach that encourages flexibility (more on this topic in Chapter 6).

The above discussion on the way in which we struggle with deriving meaning from data raises the question of how we can find our path through data. If statistical significance is flawed and human reading of data is problematic then where do we turn? The answer perhaps lies in the use of theoretical frameworks to guide our activity. These are now discussed below.

Is theory important?

This comes to the crux of the claims about big data and its impact on analysis. Some claim that with big data we don't actually need to worry about theories, theorems or scientific laws since the only thing that matters is 'what' is happening rather than 'why'.

This view first gained prominence with Chris Anderson's article in *Wired* magazine[13] in which he argued that, in the face of big data, traditional scientific method has effectively lost its value. He threw down the gauntlet on data analytics: 'We don't need new models. We can simply sift through to find meaningful correlation... It's time to ask: what can science learn from Google?'

On this basis we no longer need to really understand consumers or hold theories of human behaviour. We can simply use computing power to uncover the important patterns and trends. Indeed, in his polemic he suggests that some sciences have drifted into 'arid, speculative theorizing' with the implication that in the meantime big data is breaking new ground.

Anderson's polarized position was quickly dismissed by those saying that such an extreme position is not strictly correct, as the tools that are used for data gathering and analysis such as statistics, mathematics and computer science are based on theory. And, to be fair, he did backtrack somewhat from his rather extreme viewpoint.

And it's true that much of the commercial application of social science is fairly atheoretical – the market research community, for instance, is not known for its philosophical zeal. So to some degree should we really expect anything different from big data? And indeed much of the existing work is empirical in nature, with researchers undertaking what is fairly straightforward analysis using correlation (albeit at times quite complex correlation such as various forms of regression analysis) or using A/B testing to check which of a number of possible options will result in a positive outcome, such as more sales.

Moreover, Cukier and Mayer-Schönberger have argued[14] that 'big means we don't have to be so concerned with causality. Instead we can explore patterns in the data that provide new insights. So whilst correlations may not tell us precisely why something is happening, they nevertheless let us know that it is indeed happening'. They go on to argue that in many cases this is 'good enough' for most purposes. So if big data analysis of millions of medical records reveal that insomnia sufferers who decide to take a particular combination of vitamins and orange juice find that they get a good night's sleep, then the exact reason for this does not matter. The fact that it happened is what is important. So in their terms, 'Big data is about what, not why. We don't always need to know the cause of a phenomenon; rather, we can let data speak for itself.'

So why should we start getting distracted by theory? There are two good reasons.

Theory is there whether we like it or not

First, as we said previously, we know that any analysis currently undertaken has some form of theoretical underpinning. Note the title of a book of essays edited by media historian Lisa Gitelman:[15] '*Raw Data' is an Oxymoron*. Analytics necessarily involves making decisions: about which data to look at, what composite variables to generate, what constitutes an outlier, and so on. These decisions involve human judgement, often well-intentioned, but guided by assumptions or hypotheses concerning what is important and why. The point is that the data does not speak for itself, as Nate Silver says:[16] 'We speak for them. We imbue them with meaning.' So as such we cannot avoid theories, it's just that much of the time they are implicit rather than explicit theories of human behaviour which are driving our analysis behaviours. But nevertheless theoretical frameworks are driving our approaches.

Big data can be misleading without theory

Before we look at the practical implications of this for using data, it's helpful to remind ourselves briefly of the historical evolution of the use of theory.

Aristotle created the idea of deductive reasoning, that is, developing a hypothesis and then testing it. His book, *The Organon (The Instrument)*, was based around his philosophy on deduction. That philosophy held sway until the early 17th century, when English philosopher/scientist Francis Bacon produced a rebuttal to Aristotle called *Novum Organon* in which he argued that true scientific knowledge should instead be based on collecting facts and then drawing conclusions: 'inductive' reasoning.[17] That is, science could discover truths about nature only by empirical testing of all possible explanations for all observed phenomena.

Writing more recently in *Science News*,[18] Tom Siegfried considered that Bacon would be a fan of big data because he would have seen his 'dreams' of empirical observations realized with the avalanche of data that is now so accessible. And indeed, we are seeing examples of companies having some real success in doing just that. For example, as Jill Dyche, Vice President of Thought Leadership at SAS Visual Analytics noted, a retail chain analysed 12 years of transactions to spot possible relationships between historical purchases. They found that identifying correlations that had not hitherto been understood meant new product placements were undertaken, leading to a 16 per cent increase in shopper spend in the first month's trial.[19] Who needs theory when you get this sort of uplift?

But others, such as US physicist and systems scientist Yaneer Bar-Yam of the New England Complex Systems Institute, argue that this is very misleading.[20] Bar-Yam argues that while those in the Bacon camp would maintain that life and society are simply too complex to yield easily to theoretical models and that data has all the answers, theory is, in fact, more essential than ever for understanding complex systems. And this is because there is never enough data to satisfy the needs of a properly empirical approach because any system where there is complexity (which, as we will see in Chapter 5, is most social systems) the number of different inputs and outcomes is infinite.

So whilst having large amounts of data is of course valuable, trying to properly understand the full complexity of the world in which we live by empirical means alone is never going to be enough. Drawing sound conclusions from big data demands the framework of a comprehensive theoretical model. As Tom Siegfried writes:

> Good science does not magically emerge from massive databases; it requires extracting the valuable information from the worthless. Big data alone doesn't discriminate between the two very well. That's what theoretical models can do.

And Yaneer Bar-Yam makes a similar point when he says that:

> No empirical observation is ever as useful as a direct measure of a future observation... It is only through generalization motivated by some form of model/theory that we can use past information to address future circumstances.

This is all very well, but why is it so relevant to the commercial context? After all, we are often not looking for major advances, but just trying to find out how to sell more insurance policies or cans of baked beans. In response to this it is worth considering if we are in danger of reaching a point where big data has managed to capture the quick wins but we need to work harder to get real value. An initial flurry of activity using new techniques will always elicit early success; the question is how do you manage these processes in a way that they will continue to deliver? And this is perhaps where we need to adopt an approach that sits between the inductive and deductive camps.

A middle way

We are starting to see that a purely inductive approach is simply not going to be sufficient to leverage the real value from big data. To make sense of data we always need some form of framework. As Peter Gould says in his book *Letting the Data Speak for Themselves*,[21] (and indeed as we have noted elsewhere):

> inanimate data can never speak for themselves, and we always need to bring some conceptual framework, either intuitive and ill-formed, or tightly and formally structured, to the task of investigation, analysis and interpretation.

The way we look at data is always framed, even if the process is automated. Someone has to write the algorithm in the first place and as such the framework is simply embedded within the algorithm rather than being made explicit. Patterns in data can generate random correlations and as such interpreting them can lead to spurious conclusions. This is exacerbated by the common practice in much research but particularly in big data, that of data dredging – seeking out every possible association or model.

However, it also seems a little rigid to apply only a straight deductive approach. This was important when we lived in a world with little data and even less computing power. We are now in an environment where we are data rich and able to use massive technological capacity to link together disparate data sets which in turn generate new data and tackle questions in new ways. Rather than being bound by induction, we can use this as a starting point to help inform our analysis process. And, argues Steve Kelling and his co-authors[22] being less hidebound by theoretical models means that it is potentially easier to do interdisciplinary research with a scope that is more holistic, able to contemplate theories of entire complex systems rather than parts of them.

Rob Kitchin, in his excellent paper 'Big Data, new epistemologies and paradigm shifts',[23] suggests a new mode of data-driven science is emerging. This approach, he suggests, is more open to a hybrid combination of abductive, inductive and deductive approaches. At the outset, it is different from traditional experimental approaches in that it aims to create hypotheses and insights from the data rather than from theory. However, this is different from a straight empirical approach in that the process of exploring data is guided by a very strong theoretical understanding of the issues. So it seeks to implement a mode of induction into the process but this is then used as a form of hypothesis generation, a means to frame questions and further deductive analysis. So existing understanding is used to guide the process of knowledge discovery which is then in turn used to develop further questions and develop our understanding.

Kitchin goes on to describe how data is generated by assumptions that are underpinned by theoretical as well as practical knowledge and experience to generate appropriate insights. So data generation, processing and analysis is carried out within the guidance of a particular framework of understanding rather than testing to see if there is a relationship between all the different variables that it is possible to capture (which, as we have seen throughout this book, is pointless).

This type of decision-making, originally developed by C S Pierce,[24] is described as 'abductive'. It looks for a conclusion that makes logical sense but is not absolute in its claims. This approach is actually widely used in science as well as market research but often some of the elements of this are implicit rather than explicit and therefore not properly understood. But importantly it helps us to understand that the relationships in the data do not, to paraphrase Thomas Nagle,[25] arise from nowhere, and they do not simply speak from themselves. Rather they arise from the framework that has been deployed. And this is not the endpoint – these relationships observed in the data are then used for formulating hypotheses and deductive testing of their validity.

Concluding thoughts

If a brand has done no or little data analytics previously then inevitably there are plenty of easy gains to be made with relatively little effort or deep contextual understanding required. But as these are steadily picked off and the competition quickly erodes the temporary advantage these generated, what next? Is it a processing power arms race? One where only technology companies ultimately benefit from selling ever-enhanced processing power? Because, surely, there are bigger prizes to be won by generating more substantial and sustained differentiation through a deep understanding of human behaviour. This is about building principles that guide not just tactical activity around specific propositions but the wider company strategy. This requires the three pillars, none of which is individually sufficient:

- big data provides the test bed, the material to be examined;
- social science is the source of theoretical frameworks to explore the data;
- consumer understanding provides the all-important context to allow us to start filtering out signal from noise – the colloquial intelligence that comes from understanding consumers and market categories.

Together these form the basis of a fundamentally new approach for companies that allows them to move from tactical big data analytics to something more differentiating and strategic, something smarter.

Notes

1 Silver, Nate (2012) *The Signal and the Noise: The art and science of prediction*, Penguin

2 Meehl, P E (1990) Why summaries of research on psychological theories are often un-interpretable, *Psychological Reports* **66**, pp 195–244

3 Silver, Nate (2012) (see note 1 above)

4 Ioannidis, John (2005) Why most published research findings are false, *PLOS Medicine*, 2, e124, August [online] http://journals.plos.org/plosmedicine/article?id=10.1371/journal.pmed.0020124

5 Shah, Shvetank, Horne, Andrew and Capella, Jaime (2012) Good data won't guarantee good decisions, *Harvard Business Review*, April

6 Redman, Thomas C (2013) What separates a good data scientist from a great one, *HBR Blog Network*, January 28 [online] https://hbr.org/2013/01/the-great-data-scientist-in-fo/

7 Gilovich, Thomas (1993) *How We Know What Isn't So: Fallibility of human reason in everyday life*, Free Press

8 Falk, Ruma (1981) The perception of randomness. In Proceedings, Fifth International Conference for the Psychology of Mathematics Education, Grenoble, France; Wagenaar, W A (1972) Generation of random sequences by human subjects: A critical survey of literature, *Psychological Bulletin*, 77, pp 65–72

9 Clarke, R D (1946) An application of the Poisson distribution, *Journal of the Institute of Actuaries* (London), **72**, p 72; Johnson, D (1981) *V-1, V-2: Hitler's vengeance on London*, Stein & Day

10 Johansson, Petter, Hall, Lars, Sikström, Sverker and Olsson, A (2005) Failure to detect mismatches between intention and outcome in a simple decision task, *Science* 310 (5745), pp 116–119

11 Nassim, Nicholas Taleb (2008) *The Black Swan: The impact of the highly improbable*, Penguin

12 Kurzweil, Ray (2005) *The Singularity is Near: When humans transcend biology*, Viking Press Inc

13 Anderson, Chris (2008) The end of theory: the data deluge makes the scientific method obsolete, *Wired*, 23 June

14 Cukier, Kenneth and Mayer-Schönberger, Viktor (2013) *Big Data: A revolution that will transform how we live, work and think*, John Murray

15 Gitelman, Lisa (ed) (2013) *'Raw Data' is an Oxymoron*, The MIT Press

16 Silver, Nate (2012) (see note 1 above)

17 Inamdar, Anil (2012) 15th-century big data – what can we learn from it? *EPM Channel* [online] http://www.epmchannel.com/2012/10/19/15th-century-big-data-what-can-we-learn-from-it/

18 Siegfried, Tom (2013) Rise of big data underscores need for theory, *Science News* [online] https://www.sciencenews.org/blog/context/rise-big-data-underscores-need-theory

19 Dyche, Jill (2012) Big data 'Eurekas!' don't just happen. *Harvard Business Review Blog*. 20 November [online] http://blogs.hbr.org/cs/2012/11/eureka_doesnt_just_happen.html

20 Bar-Yam, Yaneer (2013) The limits of phenomenology: from behaviourism and drug testing to engineering design, *Cornell University Library* [online] http://arxiv.org/abs/1308.3094

21 Gould, Peter (1981) Letting the data speak for themselves, *Annals of the Association of American Geographers* 71 (2), pp 166–76

22 Kelling, S, Hochachka, W, Fink, D, Wesley, M, Riedewald, M, Caruana, R, Ballard, G and Hooker, G (2009) Data-intensive Science: A new paradigm for biodiversity studies, *BioScience* 59 (7), pp 613–20

23 Kitchin, Rob (2014) Big Data, new epistemologies and paradigm shifts, *Big Data and Society*, 1 (1), pp 1–12

24 Miller, Harvey J (2010) The data avalanche is here. Shouldn't we be digging? *Journal of Regional Science* 50 (1), pp 181–201

25 Nagle, Thomas (1986) *The View From Nowhere*, Oxford University Press

The power of prediction

05

Philip Tetlock has become well known for his study on the predictive power of the expert. In the mid-1980s he started a test that would last 20 years by gaining the agreement of 284 experts to make nearly a hundred predictions. They were asked to make specific forecasts, answering 27,450 of his questions between them. With admirable patience Tetlock then waited over 20 years to see if these predictions came true.[1]

The bad news is that they hardly ever did. When Tetlock compared the results of the experts with those of a group of undergraduates he had recruited at the time as a control group, the experts did better, but only by a very slim margin. Tetlock was perhaps being overly generous to the experts when he pointed out that while they did better than non-experts there were clearly 'limitations' to their powers of prediction.

We know from our shared cultural stories how difficult things can be to predict. From The Beatles to Harry Potter, from Enron to Google, the world is awash with examples of 'how we got it wrong'. So many times we manage to not sign the hit band or the author, fail to predict the success or failure of a company. We often make the wrong call and miss the opportunity, fumble the ball.[2]

So perhaps we should be doing what Andrew McAfee from the MIT Sloan School of Management[3] suggests, which is relying a lot less on the judgements, diagnoses and forecasts of human experts and a lot more on the outputs of hard, data-driven algorithms. He points to a wealth of studies which show that, when judgements were made in 'messy, complex, real-world' environments, data-based algorithms were more likely than experts to get it right in the majority of cases.

The problem, he argues, is that human intuitive abilities thrive only under certain prescribed conditions: environments that are regular enough to produce good feedback quickly (such as medicine) and those that offer sufficient opportunity to practise enough to give intuitive skills a solid grounding. Meeting both these conditions, unfortunately, is all too rare. Well-designed algorithms, on the other hand, can arguably incorporate feedback and results over a long time so tend to be more reliable.

The growth of data available for prediction

It is undeniable that big data offers tremendous opportunities for organizational decision-making based more on analysis and prediction than blind leaps of faith. As these huge amounts of data become available, prediction based on crunching the data has been applied to good effect across many commercial and scientific fields to identify relationships that might otherwise be elusive.

There are a growing number of examples which illustrate this trend:

- American Express analyses data to look at behaviours that may predict defaulters. The company found that people racking up large bills on their American Express card and then registering a forwarding address in Florida were likely to declare bankruptcy, taking advantage of the liberal bankruptcy laws in that state. The correlation in the data allows American Express to take action early on.[4]

- Shazam is a UK-based online service that began in 1999 by identifying the tracks and artists playing in places such as shops and fast-food outlets.[5] Now with 400 million users in 200 countries tagging songs, TV shows and advertisements, it has built up such a vast store of data on preferences it claims it has a good track record in predicting which groups/artists/songs are going to be successful.

- In 2012 the FBI in the United States was reported[6] to be asking software companies to develop tools that would enable it to mine social data for significant words, phrases or behaviour to help predict the emergence of potential criminal behaviour.

- An Indiana University study[7] in the United States has produced what it claims is a 'statistically significant' relationship between Twitter data and US election results.

- Amazon filed a patent for an algorithm based system of 'anticipatory package shipping' which predicts purchases based on shoppers' Amazon activity, including time on site, duration of views, links clicked and hovered over, shopping cart activity and wish lists. The benefits of this are to potentially reduce shipping, inventory and supply chain costs.[8]

Within many data-intensive industries such as finance, healthcare and e-commerce, large amounts of data have been available for some time on individual behaviours and outcomes. However, with the increasing datafication of our lives that we described in Chapter 1, there is far more data available than ever before in many more sectors.

This means that there is a lot of excitement about our ability to extend and improve the predictions we make. These may be quite modest predictions that have a marginal effect (eg what a web page should look like to maximize sales) but if the promise can be shown to be right, then the scale with which they are applied can surely mean substantial benefits to a brand's bottom line.

An interesting extension to this is 'nowcasting' which is increasingly being used to make short-term predictions by teasing out what is happening 'now' rather than waiting for the slower-moving, long-term indicators to become available. Google claimed that the use of Google Trends, which allows analysis of the searches undertaken by its users, can be used to good effect in this way. It has cited as an example that 'the volume of queries on automobile sales during the second week in June may be helpful in predicting the June auto sales report which is released several weeks later in July.'[9]

However, just how good are we at predicting from big data? We will look now a little more carefully at the perils and pitfalls of prediction.

How good is our ability to predict?

Although there has been a lot of excitement about the opportunity to use big data to predict future outcomes, a number of studies are questioning some of the findings.

Google Flu Trends is a good case in point. Google had originally published a paper claiming that Google searches (as evidenced by Google trends) had a 90 per cent match with the number of cases recorded by the US Center for Disease Control (CDC).[10] However, Google subsequently received a lot of publicity for over-estimating the flu trend at the beginning of 2013,[11] when it reported that 11 per cent of the US population had influenza, almost double the actual estimates by the CDC. A team of researchers led by David Lazer of Northeastern University noted that 'essentially, the methodology was to find the best matches among 50 million search terms to fit 1,152 data points.' The chances of finding search terms that seemed to match the incidence of flu but in fact were unrelated – 'were quite high'.[12] It was apparent that Google's algorithm focused on counting searches and failed to take context into account, since it was likely that increased news coverage and social media activity about flu during this period had an impact on greater online activity related to flu, rather *actual* outbreaks of flu.

And there are other examples where the initial hype has not been reflected in the subsequent data. Felix Ming Fai Wong and others at Princeton University[13] cast doubt on the propensity of Twitter to be a reliable predictor of the success of cinema films. During the 2012 Oscars season they collected 1.7 million tweets that contained the titles of 34 recently released or Oscar-nominated films. After disposing of the irrelevant tweets (about half of them), they then classified the remainder based on whether they contained either positive or negative comments and if they were tweeted after the person had seen the movie, to try to ensure that genuine opinion was collected. They also collected reviews about the very same films from the Internet Movie Database and RottenTomatoes.com.

They concluded from their research that Twitter's predictive ability is limited. So, for example, reviews on Twitter do not typically reflect the reviews that appear on other online sites. But more importantly, the Twitter data did not always translate into box office revenue (although they do point out that in some cases it can).

Daniel Gayo-Avello, at the University of Oviedo in Spain, similarly disputed the ability of Twitter to predict elections.[14] He undertook an analysis of the research done to date in this area and concluded that the assumptions underlying much of the prior research were flawed. His analysis suggested that work had generally assumed all tweets were trustworthy, representative and not affected by self-selection. All of these issues, he claims, explain why he was not able to find any papers that were able to provide a credible prediction of a future result.

These studies cast doubt on our ability to use big data to predict future behaviours. However, we should be a little careful in reaching too hasty a conclusion that big data is not useful for prediction purposes. These studies are based on social media and search engine data rather than other material such as a brand's transaction data where the story may be very different. Further, we should not rush to conclude that we cannot use this kind of data for prediction purposes; perhaps the model needs to be refined. But nevertheless these studies highlight the fact that prediction is not a straightforward matter. Exactly why this is the case is explored below.

Understanding the limitations of prediction

All predictions are only as good as the historical data they are based on – and this means that what is being predicted needs to have some form of precedent. However, many of the predictions we make simply do not have historical data that we can consider to be relevant for future projections. This may be due to records not being available (there is no historical data for a new product). And sometimes historical data may be illusory – we may have a lot of historical data related to mobile phone purchase and usage etc but the extent to which that can be used to help predict current behaviours is debatable as the category has changed so much.

There are other aspects of prediction analysis besides a lack of historical precedent where things can go wrong, as we discuss below.

Over-fitting the historical data: This usually happens when there are too many parameters used relative to the sample size. In this case, according to Nate Silver,[15] you can end up with a model that fits the noise in the data rather than the signal.

This tendency to pick and choose from a large set of data to explain a small one is also ridiculed by David J Leinweber of Caltech, who described[16] how he and his colleagues carried out an (unpublished) exercise in 1995 to highlight the risks of data mining in quantitative investing. It was able to show a strong statistical association between the annual changes in the S&P 500 stock index in the United States and butter production in Bangladesh (in total disregard of common sense, he notes). However, word of mouth soon spread this spurious correlation to the point where it ended up being included on the curriculum in some business schools. Such was the seriousness with which it was taken that Leinweber published the paper over a decade later to emphasize the spuriousness of the proposition.

Selectivity: We often tend to ignore inconvenient data points. So for example, there has been a lot of discussion about the way in which the financial meltdown in 2008 could have been avoided if financial institutions had not limited the period of time they used for their projections to those which, it often seemed, fitted conveniently with their assessments of future growth.

So prediction is not always easy, and there are definitely pitfalls that can be fallen into. But also, we need to consider if some things are inherently harder to predict than other things. In particular, we need to understand if social sciences are generally harder and more complex to navigate than the natural sciences. If they are, then this has significant implications for strategic marketers.

Why some things are easier to predict than others: complex vs simple systems

With this in mind it is important here to take a step back and look more generally at the concept of prediction. As Tim Harford sets out in his book[17] *Adapt: Why success always starts with failure*:

The problem is not the experts; it is the world they inhabit – the world we all inhabit – which is simply too complicated for anyone to analyse with much success.

Of course, we can predict some things pretty well. We tend to know that if we go on our summer vacations in the UK it will rain (I can attest to this from years of personal experience!) just as we can predict that the sun will rise in the morning. We can also predict that pretty sophisticated things will operate in a predetermined fashion so that our aircraft can be trusted to fly, birds will migrate in a predictable way and the lights in my house will go on when I flick the switch.

On the other hand, it is pretty difficult to predict with any significant level of accuracy which way share prices will move, how many people will buy a new model of car or whether a campaign encouraging healthy eating will have the desired effect.

So what determines why we can predict some things well while in other areas we are woefully inadequate? Duncan Watts describes this phenomenon as the difference between simple and complex systems:

> Simple systems are those for which a model can capture all or most of the variation in what we observe... complex systems are another animal entirely... Nobody really agrees on what makes a complex system 'complex' but it's generally accepted that complexity arises out of many interdependent components interacting in non-linear ways.[18]

So a simple system can be highly sophisticated but, importantly, we are able to model and predict the system. These can be as complex as the movement of the planets, the handling of a car or the aerodynamics of an aircraft. But because we can capture the variance in these systems and model it, then for the purposes of this analysis the systems are 'simple'. And if we can model the variance in a system, then we can predict the activity of that system.

Complex systems, by contrast, are inherently unpredictable as we cannot account for a high proportion of the variance that influences outcomes. In these circumstances, notes Watts, 'tiny disturbances in one part of the system can get amplified to produce larger effects somewhere else. There is only so much that anyone can model and predict.'

And an awful lot of social and economic activity is necessarily complex. Social science is generally not an area where we can always capture the majority of the variance and therefore predict with confidence. Of course market research companies have ingenious ways to try to keep this variance to a minimum but nevertheless we can conclude that we need to recognize that managing uncertainty is a fact of life when trying to predict much consumer behaviour.

The influence of social effects on system complexity

Part of the complexity of social and economic activity is due to the way in which social effects operate. A great example of this is a study conducted by Watts and his colleagues where they used the music downloads market to explore the social network that people were operating within.[19]

An artificial music market was created with over 14,000 consumers from a teen-related website. All participants were asked to rate a list of previously-unheard songs from unknown bands. They were required to assign a rating to the song and then given an option to download it. This corresponds to the 'individual' model of decision-making, where we are making decisions without reference to others. As might be expected, there was a normal distribution of preferences for the different songs, with the most popular songs being around three times as popular as the least popular.

The second group of individuals undertook exactly the same task but with a crucial difference: they could see the number of times that the songs had been downloaded by others. When the consumers could see the preferences of others (in the form of downloads) there was a significant shift in consumers' preferences, with just a few songs being hugely popular and the majority of songs getting much lower ratings. In this scenario the ratio between the most popular and the least popular was at least thirty to one.

And the tracks that were popular when selected individually (ie not seeing what had been downloaded) bore little relationship to the tracks selected when consumers could see what had been downloaded by others in their 'network'. So we can see that interactions between individuals ended up drastically enhancing small fluctuations to produce outcomes that would have been very difficult to predict.

So we live in a world where life is more complex than it perhaps first appears. In a complex world we need to be judicious about the extent to which we can predict with certainty.

Building models to make predictions

With this in mind, Watts suggests that perhaps the best we can do when attempting to make predictions within complex systems is to model the *probability* of particular outcomes[20] rather than providing absolute predictions. This gives the recipient a much better understanding of how robust the prediction is and as such gives guidance to the appropriate business response.

Given there is so much variance in the data then in many situations a prediction based on probabilities is perhaps as much as we can do. So while we can predict the way in which the aerodynamics of an aircraft wing will work with great confidence, trying to predict the sales volumes of a new product has much more variance and as such a probabilistic approach may well be more appropriate.

However, reporting predictions in terms of probabilities also has its issues as the study of weather forecasting illustrates – a complex system if ever there was one, particularly in the UK. Many studies have found that we are poor at dealing with probabilistic guidance:[21] we don't want to know if there is a 40 per cent chance of rain tomorrow, we definitely want to know if it will rain tomorrow so we can take appropriate action.

These same principles apply to business decisions. A product manager will generally be underwhelmed by receiving guidance saying there is a 50 per cent chance of generating sales of say, US $50million. The language traditionally demanded by the business case is way more definitive than that. Yet perhaps we need to work at better communicating in this way to avoid the inevitable overconfidence that results when providing predictions of absolute numbers within complex systems.

One of the challenges when generating predictions is that it can be hard to know in advance what is relevant to the prediction model. The sheer volume of different factors that could influence a decision makes it extremely hard to pin down at the time. If Microsoft had known, for instance, how important the internet market was to become it would have taken a different market strategy before Google captured the search market. If Nokia had been able to predict the importance of the touch screen then perhaps it too may have taken a different approach prior to Apple dominating the mobile phone market.

The point is that we often apply a 'post-hoc rationalization', as the factors relevant to a particular outcome are easy to identify in hindsight. But in reality it is very hard to pick out in advance all the factors that will drive success or failure for your proposition.

This is never more the case than in so-called 'black swan'[22] events – events that happen rarely but are of seismic importance when they do. These are events whose significance is only really understood with the benefit of historical perspective – such as the internet, mobile telephony or perhaps even the invention of the washing machine. As some categories have more black swan events than others the task of prediction in these can be tough. Scenario planning is perhaps one way in which brands can be better equipped to deal with this sort of uncertainty.

Creating scenarios to deal with uncertainty

Scenario planning is used to try to explore a number of different 'futures' in order to be as prepared for change as possible. It doesn't 'predict' as such, but provides a robust framework in which to explore alternatives to the 'official future', which is usually more comfortable, and hence more potentially misleading, than other possible futures. For example, it can act as a 'wind tunnel' to test business plans or strategies by seeing what would happen in the different scenarios.

Importantly, it offers a common vocabulary for strategic discussions about what can often be quite different views of the future within an organization.

Gill Ringland and Laurie Young[23] describe several rules of thumb about what works and what doesn't when it comes to successful scenario planning including:

- It needs a wide range of inputs to provide a useful basis for decisions. This can range from extensive desk research, horizon-scanning and interviews to scenario-building sessions with both internal and external participants.

- It's critical to decide why it is being done. If it's to act as a context for strategic decision-making rather than an exercise in building skills, supporting desk research is the important element.

Learning to live with uncertainty: the strategy paradox

There is an increasing realization that in the inherently unstable contexts in which most brands operate, attempts to make very accurate predictions are of less value and, as such, business processes need to reflect this inherent unpredictability. Indeed, the work of Michael Raynor[24] suggests there is a 'strategy paradox' whereby although companies apply excellent logic in the development of their innovation strategy, they can simply call it wrong.

Raynor uses the example of Sony's Betamax videocassette to illustrate this. According to Raynor, Sony undertook high quality analysis of the market and a strategy was developed that looked very sensible considering the explosive growth of the video rental market. Unfortunately there was a shift in consumer demand. This favoured VHS due, in part, to the longer running time being able to store full-length movies. Both Betamax and VHS were standalone formats rather than open, which meant the competing manufacturers brought down the price. This happened far more quickly than anyone in the industry had anticipated and as such the Sony position was, in hindsight, a failure.

But these issues are only failures in hindsight – history is always rewritten from the perspective of the winner. Raynor goes on to cite the example of Apple which, in some ways, had a similar position to

Sony's Betamax strategy (based on closed architecture, proprietary standards, resisted by content providers) and as with Sony it stuck to its strategy. The difference, according to Raynor, was that Sony simply happened to be wrong and Apple happened to be right.

Of course the history books write it differently as we are generally more attracted to the story of vision and leadership overcoming all the odds. Unfortunately, as Duncan Watts points out, 'whether great strategy succeeds or fails depends entirely on whether the initial vision happens to be right or not. And that is not just difficult to know in advance, but impossible.'[25]

To this end Michael Raynor advocates that brands should be adopting a strategy of flexibility, where we integrate strategic uncertainty into the planning process. So we have a broad portfolio of strategies, some of which will work and others that we recognize will fall on stony ground. This is similar to the approach proposed by Henry Mintzberg[26] of an 'emergent strategy' which suggests we should rely less on making predictions about the long-term future and focus more on reacting quickly to short-term changes on the ground.

The case study[27] that is often quoted in this context is that of Zara, the clothes retailer which has successfully developed a 'measure and react' strategy. Its success depends on its ability to measure the demands of the market, design the appropriate response, produce, ship and then sell the garment within a very short space of time. For Zara, reacting to short-term trends on the ground has been highly profitable.

The challenge for other markets is to emulate this success, although there are plenty of barriers, not least the cost of producing new products in industries where the design and production cycles are notoriously long and investment-intensive. However, it is likely that this is the new reality of the market and those companies that are able to 'measure and react' quickly and efficiently are likely to be in a position to gain competitive advantage.

Concluding thoughts

We have seen that whilst prediction is tempting, we need a better understanding of the circumstances in which it has been found to be effective and when has it failed. Big data was hailed as the answer to our business need for greater certainty – after all as humans at one level we are highly predictable. But unfortunately the reality is not that simple. Humans operate in complex, interconnected eco-systems where there are a huge number of interdependencies. It is easy to create a model that indicates the pattern of future behaviour which, once it is typed up in a presentation with a compellingly intricate set of numbers to support it, we are very tempted to believe, regardless of the veracity or otherwise. And we often look in a rear view mirror, justifying why some things were successes and other things were not, thinking we are learning the lessons but all the time engaging in post-hoc rationalization to explain the success or failure of an investment.

So what role can big data play? Is there in fact a role for big data in the prediction of human behaviour? Quite possibly yes but we need to better identify where it works and where it is less relevant. There are consistencies in some of our behaviours that allow us to use data to have some predictive value, just as survey data has long been used by market researchers to predict the take-up of services. There is certainly some value in doing so.

But perhaps we are in danger of having too great an ambition for big data to go way beyond what is feasible. When we look at data on a page it is inviting to forget that there are human beings represented by that data. And when humans are involved we are in a world of complexity where it is not necessarily as easy as we think to predict outcomes, such as the spread of human flu.

Surely the real opportunity for big data is to explain rather than necessarily predict. Because by explaining the market context we can then develop appropriate strategies for managing different possible outcomes. Betting on an apparently firm prediction from big data without understanding the human context may at times work but it could also land the business in the same place as Betamax.

Notes

1 Tetlock, Philip E (2005) *Expert Political Judgement: How good is it?* Princeton University Press

2 Parish, James Robert (2007) *Fiasco: A history of Hollywood's iconic flops*, Wiley

3 McAfee, Andrew (2014) When human judgement works well, and when it doesn't, *HBR Blog Network*, 6 January [online] https://hbr.org/2014/01/when-human-judgment-works-well-and-when-it-doesnt/

4 Bollier, Davis (2012) *The promise and perils of big data*, The Aspen Institute

5 Patrizio, Andy (2013) Shazam predicts future pop stars by analyzing listener data, *CITE World* [online] http://www.citeworld.com/consumerization/22777/shazam-data-predictions-pop-stars

6 Warman, Matt (2012) FBI to use Twitter to predict crimes, *Daily Telegraph*, 27 January

7 Meyer, Robinson (2013) A new study says Twitter can predict US elections, *The Atlantic*, 13 August

8 Ulanoff, Lance (2014) Amazon knows what you want before you buy it, *Predictive Analytics Times* [online] http://www.predictiveanalyticsworld.com/patimes/amazon-knows-what-you-want-before-you-buy-it/

9 Choi, Hyunyoung and Varian, Hal (2011) Predicting the present with Google Trends, 18 December [online] http://people.ischool.berkeley.edu/~hal/Papers/2011/ptp.pdf

10 Ginsberg, Jeremy, Mohebbi, Matthew H, Pate, Rajan S, Brammer, Lynnette, Smolinski, Mark S and Brilliant, Larry (2009) Detecting influenza epidemics using search engine query data, *Nature* 457, pp1012–14,19 February, DOI:10.1038/nature07634

11 Bilton, Nick (2013) Disruptions: data without context tells a misleading story, *New York Times*, 23 February

12 Lazer, David, Kennedy, Ryan, King, Gary and Vespignani, Alessandro (2014) The parable of google flu: traps in big data analysis, *Science* 343 (6176), pp 1203–05, DOI: 10.1126/science.1248506

13 Wong, Felix Ming Fai, Sen, Soumya and Chiang, Mung (2012) Why watching movie tweets won't tell the whole story, *WOSN '12*, Proceedings of the 2012 ACM workshop on online social networks, pp 61–66

14 Gayo-Avello, Daniel (2012) 'I wanted to predict elections with twitter and all I got was this lousy paper' – a balanced survey on election prediction using Twitter data, arXiv preprint arXiv:1204.6441

15 Silver, Nate (2011) Models can be superficial in politics, too, *New York Times*, 24 March

16 Leinweber, David J (2007) Stupid data miner tricks: overfitting the S&P 500, *The Journal of Investing*, Spring 16, (1), pp 15–22

17 Harford, Tim (2011) *Adapt: Why success always starts with failure*, Hachette

18   Watts, Duncan J (2011) *Everything is Obvious Once You Know the Answer: How common sense fails*, Atlantic Books

19   Salganik, Matthew J, Dodds, Peter Sheridan and Watts, Duncan J (2006) Experimental study of inequality and unpredictability in an artificial cultural environment, *Science* 311 (5762), pp 854–56

20   Watts, Duncan J (2011) (see note 18 above)

21   Gigerenzer, Gerd, Hertwig, Ralph, Van Den Broek, Eva, Fasolo, Barbara and Katsikopoulos, Konstantinos V (2005) 'A 30% chance of rain tomorrow': how does the public understand probabilistic weather forecasts? *Risk Analysis* 25 (3), pp 623–29, June

22   Taleb, Nassim Nicholas (2007) *The Black Swan: The impact of the highly improbable*, Random House

23   Ringland, Gill and Young, Laurie (2006) *Scenarios in Marketing: from vision to decision*, John Wiley & Sons

24   Raynor, Michael (2007) *The Strategy Paradox: Why committing to success leads to failure*, Doubleday

25   Watts, Duncan J (2011) (see note 18 above)

26   Mintzberg, Henry (2000) *The Rise and Fall of Strategic Planning*, Pearson Education

27   Ferdows, Kasra, Lewis, Michael A and Machuca, Jose A D (2004) Rapid-fire fulfillment, *Harvard Business Review Magazine*, November

The advertisers' dilemma

06

One of the main applications where the scale of investment in big data is already quite substantial – and which will be very familiar to modern marketers – is online advertising. This is hardly surprising, as brands engage in an 'arms race' to develop ever-more powerful precision tools to identify and target relevant groups of consumers.

Online advertising is now a multi-billion dollar industry and one which has long since overtaken both TV and print in most developed markets. Google alone, whose value is predicated on search-based advertising, is worth US $400 billion. This is quite a notable achievement for a company that has only been in existence since 1997.

A key characteristic of online advertising is, of course, that it is driven by big data: it uses personal data related to consumers' browsing habits, along with other information held and traded by a range of database marketing organizations and other brands. While the benefits of this sort of precision have been much discussed, the three major ones are:

- cost: relative to other media, online advertising is much cheaper for advertisers;

- measurability: advertisers can collect details of the effectiveness of the advertising using a variety of metrics such as whether the advertisement was viewed, the click-through rate, percentage of click-throughs resulting in a sale and so on;

- targeting: because of the low costs of online advertising, advertisers can focus on narrow market segments for targeted advertising.

Given the dominance of online, it is little wonder that marketers focus much of their activity in this area. A GfK/*Guardian* study explored professional marketers' response to the use of big data for online advertising.[1]

One theme apparent from the data and accompanying comments of the UK marketers who were interviewed was the opportunity that big data offered for moving marketing from a somewhat 'theoretical' practice, where it was not always possible to measure outcomes, to the 'promise of an entirely new level of understanding of the market, replacing (sometimes educated) guesswork and crude aggregation' as one of the marketers interviewed so usefully and articulately put it.

But it is the tough economic environment in which many brands have found themselves over the last few years that has sharpened the issue and been a strong influence in the enthusiastic adoption of data-driven advertising. The solution for consumers spending less is often considered to be competitive advantage through improved personalization of advertising.

As another marketer in the survey put it, consumers increasingly 'expect to have information on products or services targeted specifically at them based on their interests or demographic'. And, indeed, big data is being seen as a cost-effective option to deliver this with an expectation that 'tools to make practical use of it will become more affordable and more usable'.

That is why marketers are rushing to invest to ensure that they keep their edge in the face of competitors doing the same. One marketer rather ruefully likened this to 'racing against Lance Armstrong in the '90s'. And they appear to see little choice. Not to join in this 'arms race' feels dangerous where the losses could be high for their brand. There is a sense that marketers need to face this challenge as the tools are now available and consumers are increasingly expecting more personalized approaches.

While marketers have rushed to embrace big data for the promises of targeting it offers, perhaps not enough has been asked about what we understand about the broader context of online advertising. Surely there are two areas we need to think about more clearly. First, how do we manage the metrics associated with online advertising?

Have we got the right metrics and are we interpreting them correctly? Second, have we properly understood how online advertising works and as such should we be considering the human element of this more carefully? We deal with both elements of this important application of big data in turn below.

Online advertising metrics

Online advertising comes with a whole host of metrics that appear to make a lot of sense and have a real logic about them. But are we able to assert that online advertising works as effectively as the metrics appear to suggest? There is an increasing body of work that provides some new insights into this that are discussed below.

Advertising blocking

Consumers have a range of solutions now available to them if they wish to block online advertising. In the GfK/*Guardian* survey mentioned earlier, it was reported that 38 per cent of consumers now use some form of ad blocking, mainly via software downloads but also through changing the settings on their browsing software. A recent report on the topic titled 'The theory of peak advertising and the future of the web' by Tim Hwang and Adi Kamdar[2] suggested that the proportion of users blocking ads will continue to increase over time. This is because it is nearly costless for users. Notably, it is the users of the browsers Chrome and Firefox – which continue to gain market share – who most frequently install ad blocking software. So the projected reach of online advertising may have to be reduced over time to take into account what appears to be a growing proportion of the online population that are 'opting out'.

Advertising fraud

Hwang and Kamdar cite click fraud as a major concern, noting a case in March 2013 where fraudulent click-throughs, generated through botnets (networks of private computers infected with malicious software and controlled as a group without the owners' knowledge), were estimated to have cost display advertisers US $6 million per month. The rise in fraud clearly has the potential to curb enthusiasm for continued growth of investment.

At the very least this calls for caution in how we interpret the metrics by which we measure the success or otherwise of the online advertising. Some of the issues that Benjamin Edelman of Harvard Business School has identified[3] include:

- Banner farming: When advertisers pay by page impression (the frequency by which an online advert is seen) then it is tempting for unscrupulous perpetrators to load advertisements invisibly. A rogue 'banner farm' site can load scores of banners invisibly and get paid. The problem is that this is not always easily spotted, as even on legitimate sites click-through rates can be as low as 0.1 per cent. That makes it difficult to spot a rogue site using this measure alone.

- Pay-per-click: The sensible response to the challenge of pay-by-impression is pay-per-click on the advertisement. This is, of course, the model used for search advertising. However, here too there are challenges from 'bots', the automated programs that pose as genuine internet users. These are estimated to result in 36 per cent of all web traffic to be considered fake, according to the Interactive Advertising Bureau (IAB) trade group. So-called bot traffic cheats advertisers because marketers typically pay for ads whenever they are loaded in response to users visiting web pages, regardless of whether the users are actual people.

- Pay-per-sale: It is tempting to think that only paying when a sale is achieved is a secure means of ensuring that the right metrics are used to assess the effectiveness of advertising. However, again, this can be gamed. A cheater can identify users likely to buy from a merchant and then monitor when the user goes to the merchant's site, or they can rely on the fact that they visit them frequently. Once the user buys from that site then the cheater can claim to have referred the users and claim the commission. In 2013 two individuals pleaded guilty to taking an astonishing US $21 million from eBay's affiliate programme using these methods.

Teasing apart cause and effect

Another challenge for online advertising is trying to determine the degree to which an upturn in a brand's sales can be attributed to online advertising. The issue here is that it can be difficult to pick apart campaign effects from background effects. This is because we don't tend to use the internet in a consistent manner, rather our usage is somewhat 'lumpy' – we have periods of intense activity and other periods of low or no activity. So sometimes we like to visit a lot of different sites and perhaps make a range of purchases, other days we exhibit little or no online activity or indeed purchases. On a day where we make a lot of searches and see a lot of advertising we may well be likely to make a lot of purchases. And whilst it may be tempting to see this correlation as causal, this is not necessarily the case.

With the incidence of purchasing being so low in online advertising, it can be hard to identify a statistically-significant effect that can be attributed to the effectiveness of the advertising rather than a function of the market context.

Targeting problems when measuring effectiveness

Because the baseline probability of making a purchase (or indeed clicking through) in response to an online advertisement is so low, advertisers will naturally want to focus on the 'low-hanging fruit', those customers that are most likely to make a purchase.

However, this ignores the context as the more targeted the activity, the more likely the target group are to have made a purchase anyway. This was demonstrated in a study by Chris Nosko of Chicago University and Steven Tadelis of the University of California, Berkeley, together with Thomas Blake of eBay.[4] By experimenting with disabling some of eBay's paid search campaign, they found that returns from paid searches were only a fraction of what their standard reporting systems indicated. Many customers who clicked on the paid ads would have bought from eBay anyway, even without the paid searches. It can be argued, of course, that this is an effect that is more likely to impact better-known brands rather than ones seeking to grow awareness (as advertising is less important for awareness among larger brands).

This effect is particularly acute in relation to re-targeting: showing banner ads to those who have already visited the site. While re-targeting may increase the users' probability to purchase, the vendor cannot claim to be responsible for *all* purchases on this basis, but the incremental increase in purchase probability instead. As Benjamin Edelman dryly notes, 'Reporting... tend[s] to claim for the entire purchases of all users who see or click the targeted advertisements, not just the incremental purchases.'

So whilst we have a wide range of metrics available for assessing the effectiveness of online advertising, it is clear that their provenance needs to be properly understood in order to determine what they are actually measuring. This is not to say that they don't have value, but we need to be clear what their value is and how we should interpret them.

Psychology of online advertising

Online advertising is an interesting case study in the application of big data. At one level it looks straightforward; there appear to be clear metrics, the ability to measure the return on investment and clarity about the subsequent action that should be taken. Advertisers, one would have hoped, can at last breathe a sigh of relief after years of semi-guesswork with broadcast media. But as the above discussion shows, metrics are not always what they might seem – we need to apply a level of interpretation if we are to avoid spurious conclusions.

The other side of the story is to consider the human context of this application of big data. Again, we need to question whether the metrics are actually telling the whole story. We explore below two ways where a more nuanced perspective might generate greater understanding of the role played by online advertising.

Signalling

Consumers are always looking for short cuts – signals – when trying to decide what to buy. But a key advertising issue that is little discussed is not so much the advert's content per se but what the advert itself infers or signals about the brand.

Economist George Akerlof published a famous paper on this in 1970 called 'The market for "lemons": quality, uncertainty and the market mechanism'.[5] This deals with the way in which buyers and sellers have different information about the product. If, for example, you have a car that you are trying to sell, you probably know quite a bit about it but may not choose to disclose the oil leak and the fact that it won't start on cold mornings. Meanwhile, your neighbour is trying to sell a similar car which does not have these faults but, because your car's faults are only known to you, your neighbour cannot sell his for any higher a price than what you are willing to accept for your 'lemon'.

This causes real difficulties in markets, which may then subsequently break down. As Akerlof wrote later:[6]

> Indeed, I soon saw that asymmetric information was potentially an issue in any market where the quality of goods would be difficult to see by anything other than casual inspection. Rather than being a handful of markets, the exception rather than the rule, that seemed to me to include most markets.

Obviously regulations and guarantees can help protect against this happening in markets. Activities such as providing consumers with their own historical data such as that proposed by the UK government's midata programme can help reduce market asymmetries.[7]

But advertising also has a role to play. In a paper by Evan Davis *et al*,[8] they ask the question, 'Is advertising rational?' concluding:

> It is not so much the claims made by advertisers that are helpful, but the fact that they are willing to spend extravagant amounts of money on a product that is informative.

That means that advertising acts as a form of screening mechanism, one that's so expensive it deters low-quality sellers, while still being affordable for high-quality sellers. It signals that the product or service being advertised is believed in enough to attract investment, whether from customers buying it or investors backing the company.

Richard Kihlstrom and Michael Riordan explained this signalling logic behind advertising in a 1984 paper:[9]

> When a firm signals by advertising, it demonstrates to consumers that its production costs and the demand for its product are such that advertising costs can be recovered. In order for advertising to be an effective signal, high-quality firms must be able to recover advertising costs while low-quality firms cannot.

Because the barriers to entry have become so low with online advertising, the 'signalling problem' can be even greater as the ordinary consumer can no longer distinguish between a quality brand and the 'lemon'. There is no way to tell if they are one of a small number of people being targeted for not very much money or part of a major campaign in which a lot of money is being invested.

Perhaps this is why print continues to maintain its price premium relative to online advertising. Mary Meeker's Internet Trends 2014 presentation[10] indicates that print accounted for 5 per cent of media consumption in 2014, but 19 per cent of ad budgets. Compared to print, the value of the web as an advertising medium is staying low relative to time spent. This is perhaps in no small part due to the signalling value of appearing in a more expensive print medium.

So despite the breadth of metrics that we have at our disposal concerning advertising effectiveness, we are in danger of missing a critical piece of the jigsaw that is not so easy to pick up. And until we consider the 'human' element in the digital advertising eco-system we will underestimate the importance of this for online advertising effectiveness.

Disfluency

There is another unintended psychological side effect of online advertising that we are starting to understand. This is the sense that it is potentially making our relationships with brands a little too ubiquitous, a little too easy. This seems somewhat counter-intuitive in the face of the received wisdom that ease of accessibility to a brand can only be a good thing.

But is there a point at which the ease of the relationship works against the brand so it is in fact *less* memorable? Perhaps too frictionless a relationship can mean that consumers do not become sufficiently engaged with a brand. The idea is that a bit of 'grit' in the relationship could be a good way of keeping it alive.

The concept of fluency is important here. As psychologist Adam Alter points out,[11] a fluent thought is one that feels easy to have. So when you come across a common name, like John, or Tom, or Ted (in English-speaking markets at least), it's easy to process it. There's no difficulty in reading the name and making sense of it. At the other end of the spectrum you might come across a foreign name that you've never seen before, in which case it will be much more disfluent, or more difficult to process.

The implications of fluency and its counterpart, disfluency, are many. For example, people tend to prefer brands that are simple to pronounce. In 2006, Adam Alter and Daniel Oppenheimer[12] looked at the performance of hundreds of stocks immediately after they were listed on the financial markets between 1990 and 2004. They discovered that companies with simple names that were easy to pronounce received a greater post-release bump than companies with complex names. They also found that people not only tend to prefer politicians with simpler name but that lawyers in US firms with relatively simple names rise to partner status more quickly than their less-fluently-named colleagues. So we tend to like fluency. But is this a linear effect? Can we expect a continued increase in fluency to result in an uplift for a brand?

The experience of luxury brands suggest this is not necessarily the case, as they often use disfluency to give themselves a more memorable and exclusive feel. As Matthew Willcox, director of FCB's Institute of Decision Making points out,[13] Laphroaig malt whisky, Louis Vuitton and Häagen Dazs ice cream are all examples of brand names that mean we need to think about how we pronounce them. And this is often supported by ornate labels that make it more difficult to read the brand name, such as Chivas Regal, or use of less legible typefaces, such as Neiman Marcus.

These create the need for effort on the part of consumers. While such disfluency techniques are clearly well suited to luxury brands, they are not limited to them. Clothing company Patagonia, for instance, has famously run ads for jackets imploring consumers 'Please don't buy this jacket'.[14] This message clearly generates disfluency, thus encouraging closer examination and engagement with the environmental and sustainability issues that the brand is associated with.

So the question is whether the volume of online advertising is such that we reached a fluency tipping point whereby the ease with which we can access brands actually *decreases* our engagement. Some studies suggest that this position is not as counter-intuitive as it might first appear. In an interesting experiment, Betsy Sparrow, Jenny Liu, and Daniel Wegner[15] asked people to copy 40 memorable facts into a computer. Of the group, half were told their work would be saved on the computer; the other half were told it would be erased.

They found that those who believed the computer had saved the list of facts were much worse at remembering, essentially allowing themselves to 'off-load' their memory. As Wegner pointed out:

> It seems that the propensity for off-loading information to digital
> sources is so strong that people are often unable to fix details in their
> own thoughts when in the presence of a cyberbuddy.

The question is whether it is a huge leap to apply these findings to online advertising (and digital marketing generally). If we know where the information is online then we are less likely to be able to remember this information and have it to hand at critical points in the buying process. Which may be fine if the consumer is shopping online, but even then can they be relied on to find the information that would be helpful at this point? Or to retrieve the brand messages that you considered were so important for the consumer to remember when they are not online?

More research is needed here but it nevertheless illustrates how the value of online advertising may not be fully reflected by the metrics alone. We need to better understand the human context in which advertising is taking place in order to have a more rounded understanding of that value. As online advertising is now such a huge part of marketers' budgets, these issues merit further investigation.

Concluding thoughts

The point of this chapter is not to question whether online advertising actually works. Research by Les Binet and Peter Field explored the effectiveness of advertising in a report for the IPA[16] and found evidence to suggest that online advertising had an important role to play but within a framework that includes both short- and long-term objectives. And the market research industry has gone some way to developing controlled experimental studies to account for at least some of the measurement effects highlighted in this chapter.

Rather, the point is to question the blind faith that sometimes appears to take hold when faced when a nice neat row of sparkling numbers that indicate the effectiveness or otherwise of the online advertising campaign. Metrics can mask a wide variety of data 'sins' and there may well at times be a vested interested in these not being readily apparent.

Likewise, the psychology of online advertising can rain on the digital marketers' parade. What these issues highlighted here suggest is that there may be a short-term uplift for a brand from the advertising but what is the long-term impact on the brand? This is not something that is so easy to measure but nevertheless is very important to understand.

Notes

1 Strong, Colin (2013) The big data arms race part one: marketers' perceptions, *The Guardian* [online] http://www.theguardian.com/media-network/media-network-blog/2013/oct/04/big-data-arms-race-part-one-marketers

2 Hwang, Tim and Kamdar, Adi (2013) The Theory of Peak Advertising and the Future of the Web, 9 October [online] http://peakads.org/

3 Edelman, Benjamin (2014) Pitfalls and fraud in online advertising metrics, *Journal of Advertising Research* 54 (2)

4 Blake, Thomas, Nosko, Chris and Tadelis, Steven (2013) Consumer heterogeneity and paid search effectiveness: a large-scale field experiment, *Mimeo* [online] http://faculty.haas.berkeley.edu/stadelis/Tadelis.pdf

5   Akerlof, George A (1970) The market for lemons: quality, uncertainty and the market mechanism, *The Quarterly Journal of Economics* 84 (3), pp 488–500.

6   Akerlof, George, (2014) Writing 'The Market for Lemons': a personal interpretive essay, *Nobelprize.org* [online] http://www.nobelprize.org/nobel_prizes/economic-sciences/laureates/2001/akerlof-article.html

7   Next steps: making midata a reality, *Gov.uk* [online] https://www.gov.uk/government/news/next-steps-making-midata-a-reality

8   Davis, Evan, Kay, John and Star, Jonathan (1991) Is advertising rational? *Business Strategy Review* 2, pp 1–23

9   Kihlstrom, Richard E and Riordan, Michael H (1984) Advertising as a Signal, *Journal of Political Economy* 92, pp 427–50

10   Meeker, Mary (2014) Internet trends 2014, *KPCB* [online] http://www.kpcb.com/internet-trends

11   Alter, Adam (2014) *Drunk Tank Pink: And other unexpected forces that shape how we think, feel, and behave*, Penguin Books

12   Alter, Adam and Oppenheimer, Daniel (2006) Predicting short-term stock fluctuations by using processing fluency, *Proceedings of the National Academy of Sciences*

13   Willcox, Matthew (2013) Why a cognitive approach is key to luxury marketing, *Luxury Daily*, 26 April

14   Allchin, Josie (2013) Case study: Patagonia's 'Don't buy this jacket' campaign, *Marketing Week*, 23 January

15   Cohen, Patricia (2011) Internet use affects memory, study finds, *New York Times*, 14 July

16   Field, Peter and Binet, Les (2014) *The Long and Short of It*, Institute for Practitioners of Advertising

PART TWO
Smart thinking

Reading minds

07

All too often it seems as if the vast reservoirs of data that are available to companies are not fully exploited, with their value for creatively developing marketing strategy ignored in favour of exploiting tactical gains. But there are big opportunities for those looking at data more strategically as it allows us to see issues in completely new ways that we have not previously been able to envisage. One of the key ways to do this is by understanding the linkages that are starting to emerge between behavioural and social/psychological characteristics. And it is to this agenda that we now turn in this Part.

The value of linking data sets

The measurement of human attributes has long been the objective of psychologists, as they have sought to move from something seemingly intangible and 'slippery' into something specific and measurable. Much of the original work in this area was undertaken by Hans Eysenck in the 1940s, particularly in relation to personality for describing individual differences in behaviour.[1]

This fed neatly into the burgeoning discipline of marketing in the 1950s, with its focus on branded goods and advertising, as consumer goods companies began to grapple with more maturing and saturated markets, followed by other sectors over the next few decades. This demanded that companies know their customers – and potential customers – well enough to influence their choices since the classic task of marketing is to identify customer needs (however defined), develop a proposition to meet those needs and then set about selling the proposition to the target market.

In turn this led to the emergence of the hugely successful market research industry, which today is estimated to be worth almost US $4 billion globally, according to Esomar.[2] The industry has developed expertise in identifying consumer needs, collecting information, typically through surveys, which are essentially questionnaires administered by interviewers either face to face, over the telephone or, increasingly, online.

But what market research struggles to collect is the detailed transaction data. Consumers typically find it hard to recall what they purchased, when and where etc, especially when they were for small amounts of money. It seems that historically we could not have our cake and eat it. We can use survey methods to collect soft attitudinal data by survey methods and accept limited data. Or we use big data to understand behaviours but not have access to our needs and attitudes.

The solution has historically been to link the needs and attitudes data that market research collates with transactional data held in customer relationship management (CRM) databases. This can provide an understanding of the relationship between what people *say* and what they actually *do*.

There are clear benefits in having access to both sides of the coin. So, for example, we can identify the way in which 'softer' measures collected by survey research can determine the outcome of actual, or 'hard' behavioural measures. This essentially becomes an exercise in measuring the return on investing in driving up customer satisfaction by looking at its impact on retention, to take one instance. Or it might involve using the historical relationship between propensity to purchase and actual sales volume within a category to decide whether to invest in a new product if that relationship has been verified.

A case in point is work undertaken for a retail bank by market research firm, GfK.[3] Tens of thousands of consumers' tracking survey results were collected as part of the bank's continuing customer satisfaction tracking studies. The surveys had a range of attitudinal measures such as satisfaction with their provider and the propensity to switch. With the consumers' permission, this was matched with their CRM data (provided by the bank) both before and after the interviews in order to see the transaction data for 12 months either side of the market research survey.

It then became possible to identify the transactions with the bank that generated their attitudes at the time of the interview, or the activities that were most likely to drive customer loyalty and increase customer value (as identified by survey data). And in turn it was possible to see the effect this had on their subsequent value to the bank and indeed their propensity to churn. This combination of 'hard' transactional data with 'softer' customer attitudes moved the analysis well beyond the blunt, tactical approach of predictive analytics to a more significant understanding of the complex interdependencies between the brand's activity and customer perceptions.

What this example illustrates is the real value that can be created for brands when integrating transaction data and survey data. But what we are now starting to see is the way in which these two spheres do not need to be generated separately. The starting point in this process is being able to identify individuals.

Knowing your customers

Retailers have long been studying how their customers make decisions about what goods and services to offer. It goes back as far as the Victorian shopkeeper who was the original one-to-one relationship manager working hard to understand customers' individual tastes and quirks. This has evolved massively through to today's supermarket chains where relevant offers are increasingly based on individual shopping habits. The wealth of data provided by loyalty cards has brought a new depth to personalized offers, and of course even those who don't use them or pay by cash can still be tracked through detailed and segmented demographic data.[4]

It is the online dimension, however, that is transforming data collection. As people do more and more of their daily activity online, cookies can track their every move, while still-newer technology is getting much smarter at identifying even those who actively try to avoid being monitored or who access the web through mobile devices, which don't use cookies.

One example is a technique called fingerprinting, which can establish an individual's unique signature by looking at what plug-ins and software have been installed, the size of the screen, the time zone and other features of any particular machines.[5] A wide-ranging investigative project from MIT and Belgium's Louvain University has found that mobile phone records identify users even more accurately than their own fingerprints, even if the phone is turned off.[6] Of course, this ability does raise many concerns, not least the fact that individuals can be identified from what were considered to be anonymized records[7] (so-called re-identification techniques). Nevertheless, to a large extent people are (often albeit unwittingly) allowing themselves to be uniquely identified, if not by actual name, with a unique ID that allows them to be targeted consistently with relevant marketing materials. The objective for brands, as the next section illustrates, is to make the valuable link between particular behaviours and attitudes through our digital footprints. If we can start to understand some of the 'softer' characteristics of people from their hard behavioural data, it opens up a huge set of opportunities for marketers, because it tells them much more interesting information about their markets.

Understanding who we are from our digital exhaust

Even though there has long been a distinction between attitudinal and behavioural data in research, we can easily make inferences about people based on their behaviours in their daily lives. Retailers make broad attitudinal assertions about individuals based on their shopping behaviour, for instance. And it does seem to be a relatively uncontroversial task to predict the attitudes of someone with a basket full of organic vegetables and other healthy ingredients as opposed to someone buying pizzas and other ready meals.

But there can be caveats with this approach, particularly when you consider that a brand may only be seeing some of a person's shopping activity, not the full picture (although this is increasingly less the case). Nevertheless, in the era of big data we are beginning to be able to make more usable and realistic claims about individuals based on what they do.

As we have noted throughout this book, as more of our lives move online, our digital exhaust says ever more about us. But whilst we will generally be aware that our activities are being tracked, we probably have less visibility of the information that is being derived from this. Perhaps this is because much of this is undertaken by brands on a proprietary basis – where there is a vested interest in the general public not having a real awareness of the full extent of what is known about them.

But a study by Cambridge University and the Microsoft Research Centre has allowed us to 'look behind the curtain' and start to understand the extent to which inferences from behavioural data can be used to predict a variety of personal attributes including religion, politics, race and sexual orientation.

Their research[8] involved 58,000 Facebook users in the United States who completed a psychometric questionnaire through the Facebook app 'myPersonality'. Those taking the test were asked to provide the researchers with access to their Facebook data. This gave the team an immensely rich data source to work with, allowing them to link the results of the personality test and demographic profiles with a person's Facebook 'Likes'.

The team were able to create some highly predictive models using these Likes. For example, they were able to identify male sexuality and sort African-Americans from Caucasian Americans, Christians from Muslims and Republicans from Democrats. There were also some pretty impressive figures for predicting relationship status and substance abuse. And not all the Likes that were used for modelling necessarily explicitly referenced the outcomes. So, for example, we would not have anticipated that liking curly fries correlated with high intelligence, or that people who liked *The Dark Knight* movie tend to be less sociable. In fact, there were relatively few obvious Likes to work with: fewer than five per cent of gay Facebook users in the study had 'liked' gay marriage, for instance.

And there are other examples. A study by researchers at Cornell University,[9] analysed over 1.5 million geotagged tweets from almost 10,000 people in the United States. They wanted to understand if the content of the tweets themselves could be used to predict the location of the user, as identified from the geotagging. So they divided the data set in two, using 90 per cent of the tweets to train their algorithm and the remaining 10 per cent to test it against. What they found was that tweets contained a lot of information about the likely location of the user. Some of it was obvious, such as tweets that were generated by the location-based social networking site Foursquare, thus giving exact location. Other tweets contained references to the city they were in. And others made reference to events that were taking place in their location. As a result of all this information, they were able to create an algorithm that correctly identifies people's home cities 68 per cent of the time, their home state 70 per cent of the time and their time zone 80 per cent of the time.

Further, a paper published in *Nature*[10] found that the lifestyles of mobile phone users could be identified from their patterns of movement. This was based on an analysis of mobile phone location data, using the data automatically generated as the device pings the network at regular intervals, regardless of whether it is in use or not. The analysis found it was possible to allocate to 95 per cent of users a unique 'fingerprint' based on their movements, so that it was possible to predict at what time of the day individuals would be in a certain neighbourhood or town. When linking this information to mapping data, it was then possible to infer a lot about that individual's lifestyle.

So what are the commercial implications of these studies? Well, the more we know about a consumer the better we are able to design products and services to meet their needs. And the human attributes (personality and demographics) identified in these studies have generally been shown to be predictive of consumer behaviour. So by identifying personality or lifestyle attributes an online movie service, for example, could potentially use it to optimize recommendations, or an online grocery store could identify appropriate promotions.

This perhaps heralds a shift in the way that big data analysis is currently conducted, much of which is atheoretical. The current argument is that there is no need for an understanding of the consumer when we can simply use predictive analytics to identify what someone will do in the future. If we know that people who buy muesli are also likely to buy pesto sauce and Pop Tarts then do we need to know anything more? Surely these findings start to show how a more nuanced understanding of consumers themselves, rather than simply their behaviours, is possible and indeed of value.

Let's return to Hans Eysenck, mentioned at the beginning of this book, who used the tools available when he was doing his research in the 1940s to start to identify unique 'factors' of personality. At the time he didn't, of course, have access to online browsing behaviour but instead used paper and pencil tests administered to hospitalized soldiers in World War II.

In terms of the standards of the time these probably seemed highly data-intensive, but by today's they seem to be somewhat limited in scale. A typical study, for example, consisted of a 39×39 matrix of 741 inter-correlations based on answers to questionnaires from 700 soldiers classed as neurotic.

In principle, we should be able to start finding new dimensions from big data that have hitherto not been explored that are useful to marketers. After all, if you have identified a new human characteristic with its own attendant needs then this surely provides a huge opportunity for the brand to differentiate itself.

The evolution of segmentation

Working on the basis that we can derive attitudinal and lifestyle information about consumers from their behavioural data also has some significant implications for marketing segmentations. Of course customer segmentation has long been a core element of the marketer's toolkit. It has been an essential means of generating an understanding of the market in which a brand operates by establishing the behaviours, needs and attitudes of different consumer groups or segments. Significantly, this enables marketers to decide which parts of the market are more attractive than others, and where to focus their activities. It also forms the basis of all the different aspects of the marketing mix, from new product development through to customer service.

There is, however, a growing debate about the future of this technique as increasing information on individuals, combined with the digitization/customization of services, is enabling the delivery of services on a one-to-one basis. Indeed, this has led IBM's CEO, Ginni Rometty, to claim that 'The shift is to go from the segment to the individual. It spells the death of the average customer.'[11]

While there may be some truth to this, what it perhaps does is reveal the way that big data analysis is often seen as a tactical activity, rather than something that can give the strategically-minded marketer an understanding of the market they would not have been able to achieve by any other means.

Indeed, perhaps one of the real breakthroughs is the way in which big data is beginning to contribute to the development of exciting new segmentation insights. Before exploring that, however, let's briefly visit some of the essential tenets of this approach to understanding consumers.

A market segmentation is assumed to be a representative, comprehensive view of 'the market', which can be a brand's customer base or the entire addressable market. While it is a straightforward task to ensure that you have your *target population* represented, it is much less easy to consider whether the needs of different stakeholders are addressed within it. For example:

- Does the customer service team get as much value from the segmentation as the product development team?

- Can it be used to help make pricing decisions or establish how best to manage channels to market?

- How can it focus advertising communications and spend?

The strength of a segmentation in providing a coherent market landscape to the marketer all too often becomes its weakness in trying to meet the needs of all relevant stakeholders. And, in this process, what is often forgotten is that any segmentation can only ever be *one* view of the market based on the data that is collected and the manner in which it is analysed.

Understandably, organizations typically want to have a single view of the market to ensure that all the different groups across the organization are working in the same direction. But the process of trying to then modify the segmentation to meet the needs of all the different stakeholder groups can mean that the end result is a set of carefully-crafted compromises. In the worst case this can result in lack of acceptance and take-up across the organization, with individual stakeholder groups creating their own segmentations to meet their specific needs (and in an uncoordinated manner).

So what is the relevance of this discussion to the availability of new data sets at the disposal of marketers? Consumer segmentation is typically developed using market research, involving a large-scale programme of interviewing a representative sample of the target population. This involves formulating a questionnaire covering, at its core, behaviours, attitudes and needs. So, for example, a segmentation designed to identify new product development opportunities will often be based around consumer needs, whereas a segmentation designed to identify particular individuals for cross-selling and maximizing current opportunities will require a more behavioural stance. A focus on brand positioning and messaging, meanwhile, will call for an attitudinal-based segmentation.

The point is that one solution will always be a compromise between the different needs of stakeholder groups across an organization.

But surely what this chapter has illustrated is the way in which big data allows us to start having a much more flexible view of the market. If we can derive information about consumer attitudes and needs from behavioural data then there is less need to undertake survey work. And as such, this creates a lot more flexibility for the consumer researcher. The distinction between behaviours and attitudes starts to be redefined so we can much more easily see the linkages between them. We can more easily generate different versions of the same segmentation for different stakeholder groups. We can also take into account something we realize increasingly: that human behaviour is 'context'-dependent and as such we may create different segments for different environments (whilst understanding how these interrelate). Yet, importantly, all the while still using the same big data set.

It is tempting to think of segmentation as an historical artefact from a time when the only marketing tools possible were to meet the needs of a group of consumers rather than tailored to individual needs. Instead, it is argued, there are very real strategic marketing benefits for understanding the structure of the market in which brands operate. But new forms of big data analytics give a new lease of life to this tool, allowing us much more flexibility and insight into how markets work.

Concluding thoughts

We started this chapter by looking at the ways in which marketers have long linked behavioural and attitudinal data, often to good – albeit limited – effect. So with segmentation studies, trade-offs are typically needed to determine the extent to which we want to focus on attitudes versus the extent to which we look at the world through the lens of behaviours. We can't have our cake and eat it.

Perhaps, that is, until now. The Facebook Likes study was one of the first to demonstrate how we can derive insights into human personal and social attributes from blunt behaviours; we no longer need to think of these as entirely separate. So as this area develops we may be able to create a much more granular, context-dependant understanding of humans that is not reliant on conducting market research surveys. We are not as constrained by expensive data gathering. We do not need to use obtrusive means to gather information that is provided naturalistically.

Of course there is a long way to go. This is an area that has yet to properly develop and evolve a sense of a shared discipline. There are the inklings of this with the emerging practice of cyber-psychology for example. And this is a huge opportunity for the market research industry to expand its repertoire to include an analysis of data that allows us to move beyond basic lifestyle inferences and into much more nuanced understanding of consumers.

Notes

1 Eysenck, H J (1947) *Dimensions of personality*, Routledge & Kegan Paul

2 Esomar, *Global Market Research 2013*, An ESOMAR Industry Report, in cooperation with BDO Accountants and Advisors [online] http://www.esomar.org/web/research_papers/book.php?id=2492

3 Strong, Colin (2013) Big data: the marketing opportunity, *Admap*, September

4 Ferguson, Donna (2013) How supermarkets get your data – and what they do with it, *The Guardian*, 8 June

5 Tanner, Adam (2013) The web cookie is dying: here's the creepier technology that comes next, *Forbes*, 17 June

6 Ungerleider, Neal (2013) Mobile phones have fingerprints, too, *Fast Company*, 29 March

7 Van Rijmenam, Mark (2013) Re-identifying anonymous people with big data, *BigData-Startups.com*, 11 February [online] http://www.bigdata-startups.com/re-identifying-anonymous-people-with-big-data/

8 Digital records could expose intimate details and personality traits of millions, *University of Cambridge* 11 March 2013 [online] http://www.cam.ac.uk/research/news/digital-records-could-expose-intimate-details-and-personality-traits-of-millions

9 How your tweets reveal your home location, *MIT Technology Review* 21 March 2014 [online] http://m.technologyreview.com/view/525741/how-your-tweets-reveal-your-home-location/

10 De Montjoye, Y, Hildage, C, Verleysen, M and Blondel, V (2013) Unique in the crowd: the privacy bounds of human mobility, *Nature* [online] http://www.nature.com/srep/2013/130325/srep01376/full/srep01376.html

11 IBM's CEO on data, the death of segmentation and the 18-month deadline, *Marketing*, 13 February 2013 [online] http://www.marketingmag.com.au/news/ibms-ceo-on-data-the-death-of-segmentation-and-the-18-month-deadline-36359/#.VGljNPnF_4I

The ties that bind

08

The previous chapter explored how access to far greater reservoirs of data is enabling marketers to gain a much deeper understanding of individual consumers. This chapter examines the way in which big data provides us with an opportunity to understand the way in which our social ties shape our behaviours.

Let's start by considering how we make decisions and what influences us to make choices. We are now living in a society where social influence and, more specifically, 'network effects', have a huge impact on each of us in many spheres of our lives, from the partners we choose and the careers we develop through to the goods and services that we purchase.[1] By networks we mean the pattern of social relationships we have with those around us.

We have, of course, always lived in a world where our values, choices and behaviours are influenced by others. It's well understood that this is part of our human experience as social animals. And this is often integral to the work of marketers and policy makers, who have long been aware that social influences are a powerful way to shape our lives.

There is, however, an increasing recognition that these social forces are more important than ever, not least due to the nature of the world we now inhabit. It is estimated that in 1800 just 3 per cent of the world's population lived in urban areas. Today this estimate has grown to more than half. This trend towards urbanization is even more pronounced in emerging markets as evidenced by the huge growth in cities such as São Paulo or Mexico City. Globalization has led to a familiarity with people's lives in what were previously isolated parts of the world. Russian and Chinese people are much more familiar with the lives of their Western counterparts and vice versa.

The significant factor is that we are now more connected than ever before in our communications. Over the course of the last century television swept into our houses and telephones became ubiquitous. In the past 10–15 years mobile phones and the internet have massively changed the communications landscape: we are now communicating and connecting on unprecedented levels.

This means we are in a position where we have 'far greater knowledge of the choices, decisions and behaviours of other people'.[2] The question we need to answer is how this much-enhanced awareness changes the way we think about and operate in the world.

While the science of networks has been around for some time, it is only recently that we have started to understand the ways in which this is relevant to the consumer purchase journey and to determine the appropriate responses for marketers, thanks to the work of people such as Paul Ormerod and Mark Earls.[3] While we now know enough to see that it is important to have some initial guidance to this landscape, it is only just creeping out of academic institutions into the commercial mainstream. As such, we need to understand how we can use big data to take advantage of the undoubted opportunities that this field offers.

Why making choices can be so difficult

Alongside the huge increase in connectedness that we now experience, there has been a phenomenal boom in the scale and scope of choices made available to us. Eric Beinhocker points out in his book *The Origin of Wealth* that the number of choices available to someone living in New York is in a different order to any other time in history:

> The Wal-Mart near John F. Kennedy Airport has over 100,000 different items in stock, there are over 200 television channels offered on cable TV, Barnes and Noble lists over 8 million titles, the local supermarket has 257 varieties of breakfast cereal, the typical department store offers 150 types of lipstick and there are over 50,000 restaurants in New York City alone.[4]

This proliferation of choice inevitably results in information overload. So how do we cut through this mass of information to arrive at the 'right decision'? In his book, *Positive Linking*, Paul Ormerod cites the social scientist Herbert Simon[5] and his reflections on whether humans, in any environment, were in fact capable of making an 'optimal' choice for three reasons:

- First, there is so much information available for social and economic decisions that could viably be considered pertinent to a particular choice that it is impossible for any individual to gather this all together. Clearly, in hindsight, it is possible to identify what would have been the right information to use to make the right choice but it is very hard to do it in advance.

- The second challenge to 'making the right decision' is our ability to generate the optimal choice, even if we have all the information available to us. As behavioural economics has recently so clearly demonstrated to us through the work of people such as Nobel Prize-winner Daniel Khaneman,[6] we typically lack the capabilities to compute the 'best' choice from the information that is presented to us. Our processing capacities are vulnerable to influences that are very difficult to disentangle and as such much of the time we are making decisions that are not always consistent or indeed 'optimal'.

- But the fundamental challenge posed by Simon is that in real-life situations optimal choice can never in fact be identified. To illustrate this he uses the example of a chess game where players have complete information (the rules of the game are fixed, the purpose is clear and each side can see what the other has done). However, even where everything is 'known' there is an almost infinite amount of possible variations and in the real world we cannot possibly know all the different parameters that the chess players have available to them.

So it is clear that we are in a position where we have imperfect information and limited computational capabilities in the context of a world where the different options are seemingly infinite. Humans, as Ormerod puts it, 'can rarely if ever know in advance with any reliable degree of accuracy the consequences of their actions. They only have the vaguest idea.'[7]

Simplifying decision-making

Nevertheless, we make decisions. And behavioural economics has demonstrated that we employ an immense number of strategies to make it easier to take decisions. A good example of this is 'fast and frugal decision making' – how we behave frugally by employing as few pieces of information as possible to make a decision as fast as possible. We return to this theme in Chapter 12.

Another way in which we ease the process of decision-making was identified by Keynes, who wrote in 1937 that a good 'rule of thumb' is to copy other people, basing your decision on the actions of others you are aware of. Keynes said 'knowing that our individual judgement is worthless, we endeavour to fall back on the judgement of the rest of the world, which is perhaps better informed'.[8]

And copying makes sense in many circumstances. Imagine you are in a small town on holiday and trying to decide which of a number of restaurants to dine in that evening. The menus appear similar, prices are very close and each has an attractive appearance. However, one restaurant has far more diners already sitting in there than the others. So which do you choose? Easy, it's the one with more diners. You are relying on the information of others to inform your decision. So it is not *mindless* copying; rather, it is copying that draws rational inferences from limited information.

We manage our lives using an infinite number of unwritten rules. Even the simplest of tasks has a complex set of social interactions that are almost automatic and unconscious for us but for which there is a shared meaning and understanding. Our lives are ruled by this rich tapestry of social meanings that are so implicit that we tend to call them 'common sense'.[9]

Moreover, as humans we also make decisions that reflect our self-interest. As economists might say, we operate in a way that optimizes the incentives we receive. This is what much of consumer research focuses upon: identifying what the consumer preferences, attitudes and needs are. That helps shape the proposition that is being developed, be it a call centre experience, a new device, different type of packaging, pricing and so on.

There is, however, an increasing awareness of the influence of *social effects* on the way in which we make decisions. A great example of this is the study of music in the downloads market conducted by Duncan Watts and his colleagues that was outlined in Chapter 6. They explore the tension between individual decision-making and the influence of social effects, in other words the social network, that people were operating within.[10] And as we will outline later, big data offers us significant new opportunities for exploring these social effects.

The role of influence and 'influencers'

There is something compelling about the idea that the opinion of some people matters more than others. It has an attractive simplicity and authenticity. After all, we all know an 'Influential', or someone who appears to be at the centre of the action, who has great taste, and gives good advice. So no wonder this idea has long captured the imagination of the marketing community: if only you could identify those key individuals and target them, then surely you would have a much more effective marketing programme.

A number of other authors have written about this phenomenon, including Malcolm Gladwell who brought the concept firmly into the public eye with *The Tipping Point*, in which a vast array of social trends were attributed to Influentials. This was the so-called 'law of the few'.[11] Gladwell cited an experiment by psychologist Stanley Milgram[12] which tested the way in which messages propagate through social networks.

Milgram recruited 300 people, two hundred of whom were based in Ohama, Nebraska and one hundred in Boston, Massachusetts. All recruits were tasked with trying to reach a named friend of Milgram's, who lived in Boston, by contacting someone from within their immediate social network. That person in turn had to find someone else on the same basis and so on. Of the 300 starting points, 64 of the chains made it to Milgram's friend and the average length of the chain was about six. A relatively high proportion of the chains went through a single person, 'Mr Jacobs', a neighbour of the target. Gladwell used this evidence to argue that a small number of people have a disproportionately larger number of contacts than others and thus exert greater influence.

More recent work, however, has called into question the idea that highly connected individuals are responsible for the contagion of ideas, attitudes and behaviours. Duncan Watts explores this is in his book *Everything is Obvious*.[13] With the help of colleagues, he replicated Milgram's work using email. After finding no equivalent to 'Mr Jacobs' in this study, Watts went on to lead the challenge against this concept of the Influential. While accepting some individuals are more influential than others, he used computer modelling to examine the power of these people to propagate trends.[14] He found that under most conditions these 'Influentials' were indeed more effective than average in starting fashions. Their importance, however, relative to others, was far less than Gladwell's 'law of the few' would have predicted.

In order for the concept of Influentials to explain shifts in behaviours and attitudes within a population, Watts identified that these highly-connected individuals would need to affect not only their own contacts, but also the connections of these contacts in turn. Influentials needed to have a multiplier effect for the maths of 'contagion' to work. But, in fact, they had no more of such an effect than the general population.

In other words, it is not just the social effect of individual to individual that causes the tipping point. It is the effect of the *network* as a whole. Watts believes this is because a trend's success depends not on the person who starts it, but on how susceptible the society is overall to the trend:

> Trends are more like forest fires: there are thousands a year, but only a few become roaring monsters. That's because in those rare situations, the landscape was ripe... If these conditions exist, any old match will do.[15]

His work on influence and networks over the years has led him to advocate what he has called the 'big seed' approach which, perhaps ironically, marries the principles of mass marketing with the impact of viral marketing. What marketers should do, he argues, is reach a lot of people through mass media, and then do what they can to enable consumers to pass the message along.

In an article in *Harvard Business Review*,[16] Watts and his co-authors pointed out that these big seed campaigns were not just hypothetical but had been successfully run using open-source software called ForwardTrack, developed by a company called Eyebeam, for a range of both commercial and non-commercial projects.

For example, in 2004 the father of one of the victims of the 1999 Columbine school shootings in the United States started an online petition for gun control in his son's name. Run in conjunction with advertising by two prominent gun control organizations, the results tracked by the software showed audience size more than doubled.

Consumer goods giant Procter & Gamble incorporated the ForwardTrack software into a viral campaign for one of its washing detergents brands. Because it was aimed at a large 'seed' of over 900,000 consumers, it is claimed that the Tide Coldwater Challenges reached an additional 40,000 people.

It's fair to say that although billions of dollars have probably been spent of trying to identify Influentials, these sorts of network-based marketing activities have not reached a mainstream marketer's audience. Nevertheless big data creates just these opportunities to understand how networks operate and for brands to create differentiation in the process. So let's explore how these can work in a little more detail.

Identifying network effects

Network science is a huge field that has grown rapidly over the past 10 to 15 years, in part because the amount of data available has grown exponentially. Paul Ormerod considers there are three types of network that are most useful to explain social and economic behaviours and attitudes:

- Scale-free networks: These are networks where most people have a small number of connections but a few have a large number of connections. This can be represented graphically as a 'hub and spokes'. Those in the hubs may (or may not) be particularly influential, but the large number of connections they possess is important in driving change. This is the closest to Gladwell's theory[17] in that a small number of people can have a disproportionate influence on the market, but is clearly more nuanced than his description.

- Small-world networks:[18] These can be described as 'overlapping groups of friends of friends'.[19] These groups are typically closely connected with a few people having long-range connections to other groups. In order to drive change it would thus be important to identify the 'long-range connectors'. It's worth pointing out, though, that the 'long-range connectors' don't necessarily have any special properties: they just happen to have connections to another group.

- Random networks: These are groups where there are no consistent patterns in how members are connected. It is a purely random assortment of connections. The common cold, for example, is transmitted through this type of network.

Most of the time networks are 'robust'. This is another way of saying that for much of the time significant change does not happen. Occasionally, however, very big changes occur where significant numbers of consumers in the network 'copy' each other. We describe these networks as 'fragile'.

The 'robust but fragile' nature of networks helps to explain why change can be difficult to implement. Much of the time networks effectively resist change but when they do become fragile it can have significant consequences. This suggests that the success of a proposition can have less to do with the fine tuning of the features, pricing, etc, and more with the way in which copying has spread across the network. This is what brand owners and their agency partners often face when they try to generate forced viral campaigns which, much of the time, simply do not succeed.

The implications of networks for marketing

If networks are in operation (ie this is a category where people effectively 'copy' each other) then the impact on performance can be made much stronger by exploiting network effects. It is surprisingly easy to observe whether network effects are influencing behaviour or attitudes in any given situation. Where consumers are forming their needs independently of others, we expect to see a normal distribution of those needs and behaviours. This is the classic bell-shaped curve. However, this becomes skewed when network effects are in operation and people are responding to the choices of others (as we saw with the music downloads study discussed in Chapter 6). Although, of course, other factors can cause a skewed distribution, which is typically related to an unequal opportunity for consumers to make a purchase – marketing controls that exist in some countries, for example.

However, as we have already seen, attempting to generate change in networks can be an uncertain business. Ormerod suggests a number of broad strategies that can be used to facilitate change, based on his model of networks described earlier:

- Scale-free networks: In these networks there is a need to identify well-connected individuals and try to induce them to change their behaviours. This can be tricky since, although they are well-connected, they are not necessarily identifiable.

- Small-world networks: These are similar to random networks, where there is a need to persuade a critical mass of consumers. But it's also important to target the individuals who link these disparate groups.

- Random networks: The requirement here is to persuade a sufficient number of people to change until a critical mass is reached where there will be a larger-scale cascade. While it is possible to predict the point at which this critical mass is reached, decisions have to be made about whether there are sufficient resources to commit to changing the views of a sufficient number of individuals to trigger this cascade.

We know that it is in the nature of the world that most outcomes are unequal. A few products get chosen many times, while most products and services are chosen infrequently. We take the 'long tail' for granted in today's world. Nevertheless, the significance of managing networks effects is that they can provide marketers with a completely new way to encourage the spread of change. They can also help to explain why the majority of product launches fail, why some marketing campaigns are less successful than others or why some products are wildly more popular than others of comparable quality.

Network effects have the potential to make a good proposition hugely popular but they also have the potential to sink a perfectly decent one. In some instances it takes only a relatively small number of consumers to transform the wider network. In others the network remains unchangeable and will not work in a brand's favour. Unfortunately, we simply have less control over contexts in which networks effects have a significant influence.

But the good news is that despite this lack of predictability, we are learning to employ systematic approaches that involve checking progress to identify which proposition will be the most popular early on. Then we amend the marketing strategy as appropriate. Careful allocation of resources used intelligently over time is the nature of the challenge in contrast to launching large-scale 'one-hit' campaigns and hoping for the best, returning to the theme we highlighted in Chapter 5.

Exploring the importance of social relationships

This chapter has focused on the very promising area of understanding the way in which networks operate and the opportunities this presents for brands. But there has been a huge amount of academic research on social relationships more generally through the use of big data. Scott Golder and Michael Macy summarize much of this in their paper. Some of the key studies they cite (which may be of particular interest to marketers) include:

- Eagle *et al* (2010) used caller behaviour (so-called metadata) among 65 million phone subscribers to show that the diversity in the social relationships of the members of a community was related to economic prosperity.[20]

- Leskovec and Horvitz (2008) researched a global instant messenger network of 240 million users to understand the degree of separation between individuals as originally measured by Stanley Milgram (as mentioned earlier). They found a mean path of 6.6 steps, relatively close to that of Milgram's 5.2.[21]

- Bakshy et al (2012) explored the way in which information spread across networks. They used news feed posts for 250 million Facebook users to show that new information spread mainly through 'weak ties'.[22]

- Bacstrom et al (2006) investigated the role of social influence on joining a community and attending events.[23]

- Ugander et al (2011) used Facebook internal data on email usage to explore the way in which a user would accept an invitation as a function of the degree of connectedness with the inviter.[24]

- Cha et al's (2010) study of 1.7 billion tweets found that 'hubs are not necessarily influential in terms of spawning retweets or mentions'.[25]

Golder and Macey's paper[26] is an excellent review of much of the recent work in this area and is a recommended read to spark ideas on ways in which this kind of analysis can have relevance and value for brands. And these examples are highly relevant to brands. Just think of how many billions of advertising dollars have been spent on targeting so-called Influentials, when studies are casting doubt on this theory.

Concluding thoughts

Social effects require us to see the world in a fundamentally different way to our Western, individualistic perspective. As such we have tended to morph it into something that is easier to understand. So instead of seeing the importance of the 'network' brands seek out 'Influentials', seeing the nature of the influence as being in the individual rather than in the structure of the network in which an Influential happens to sit.

This is partly because of our perspective on the world but also because of our measurement tools. As mentioned in Chapter 1, our ability to collect relational data has historically necessarily been through direct contact and therefore generally limited studies of social interactions to small bounded groups such as clubs and villages. But big data has changed all that. We can now develop an understanding of relationships and the effect of these relationships on consumer behaviour in a way that we would never have previously imagined.

This creates a real opportunity for differentiation, for brands to achieve cut-through in a crowded world. But it will take work. This is still something of a Cinderella subject for many organizations and most marketers have little enthusiasm for embracing something that is an intellectual stretch, not because they cannot understand it but because they have their work cut out persuading the rest of the organization. This is particularly heightened at a time when the current big data agenda at times seems so highly reductionist and individualistic. But the brand that recognizes the potential of this and makes a serious investment to use big data to unravel the nature of social effects for their business may well be one to generate real differentiation and value.

Notes

1 For further discussion of these issues see Christakis, Nicholas and Fowler, James (2011) *Connected: The amazing power of social networks and how they shape our lives*, HarperPress

2 Ormerod, Paul (2012) *Positive Linking: How networks can revolutionise the world*, Faber and Faber

3 Earls, Mark (2009) *Herd: How to change mass behaviour by harnessing our true nature*, Wiley

4 Beinhocker, Eric (2007) *The Origin of Wealth: Evolution, complexity, and the radical remaking of economics*, Random House Business

5 Simon, Herbert (1957) A Behavioural Model of Rational Choice, in *Models of Man, Social and Rational: Mathematical essays on rational human behaviour in a social setting*, Wiley

6 Khaneman, Daniel (2012) *Thinking, Fast and Slow*, Penguin

7 Ormerod, Paul (2012) (see note 2 above)

8 Keynes, John Maynard (1937) The General Theory on Employment, *The Quarterly Journal of Economics* **51** (2), pp 209–23

9 For more discussion on this issue see Watts, Duncan J (2011) *Everything is Obvious Once You Know the Answer: How common sense fails*, Atlantic Books

10 Salganik, Matthew J, Dodds, Peter Sheridan and Watts, Duncan J (2006) Experimental study of inequality and unpredictability in an artificial cultural environment, *Science* **311** (5762), pp 854–56

11 Gladwell, Malcolm (2000) *The Tipping Point: How little things can make a big difference*, Little Brown

12 Milgram, Stanley (1969) *Obedience to Authority*, Harper and Row

13 Watts, Duncan J (2011) (see note 9 above)

14 Watts, Duncan J and Dodds, Peter S (2007) Networks, influence, and public opinion formation, *Journal of Consumer Research* **34**(4), pp 441–58

15 Thompson, Clive (2008) Is the Tipping Point Toast? *Fast Company* [online] http://www.fastcompany.com/641124/tipping-point-toast

16 Watts, Duncan J, Peretti, Jonah and Frumin, Michael (2007) Viral marketing for the real world, *Harvard Business Review*, May

17 Gladwell, Malcolm (2000) (see note 11 above)

18 Watts, D J and Strogatz, S H (1998) Collective dynamics of 'small-world' networks' *Nature* **393** (6684), pp 440–42

19 Ormerod, Paul (2012) (see note 2 above)

20 Eagle, N, Macy, M W and Claxton, R (2010) Network diversity and economic development, *Science* **328**, pp1029–31

21 Leskovec, J and Horvitz, E (2008) Planetary-scale views on a large instant-messaging network, Proc.*17th Int. Conf World Wide Web*, pp 915–24, New York

22 Bakshy, E, Hofman, J M, Mason, W A and Watts, D J (2011) Everyone's an influencer: quantifying influence on Twitter. Proc. *4th ACM Int. Conf. Web Search Data Min*, pp 65–74, New York: ACM

23 Backstrom, L, Huttenlocher, D, Kleinberg J and Lan, X (2006) Group formation in large social networks: membership, growth and evolution. Proc. *12th ACM SIGKDD Int. Conf. Knowl. Discov. Data Min*, pp 44–54, New York: ACM

24 Ugander, J, Karrer, B, Backstrom, L and Marlow, C (2011) The anatomy of the Facebook social graph [online] http://arxiv.org/abs/1111.4503

25 Cha, M, Haddadi, H, Benevenuto, F and Gummadi, K P (2010) Measuring user influence in Twitter: the million follower fallacy. Proc. *4th Int. AAAI Conf. Weblogs Soc. Media*, pp 10–17, Menlo Park, CA: AAAI

26 Golder, Scott A and Macy, Michael W (2014) Digital footprints: opportunities and challenges for online social research, *Annual Review of Sociology* 40, pp 129–52

Culture shift

09

As discussed in previous chapters, we can increasingly datafy aspects of life we never thought possible, and this allows us to start seeing the world from a different perspective. One of the most ambitious examples of this is the datafying of cultural trends.

Historically cultural theory has been almost exclusively confined to academics and has been very qualitative in nature. But we are now beginning to have the opportunity to think about culture in a totally different way by studying some of the fundamental themes based on actual data. The hope is that this will enable us to be more robust in the way we understand and explore culture and how it changes and develops over time.

This might not prove to be an immediate solution to the problems that tax marketers, but is nevertheless worth further investigation so as to understand the context and relevance. This chapter will examine some of the work that has gone on in using data to understand culture in its broadest sense, from visual and literal to aural.

Seeing the world in new ways

Well before big data emerged, one of the more interesting early forays into deconstructing culture was the work of linguist George Zipf. He was struck by the frequency with which people used certain words and in 1949 came to a surprising conclusion. He discovered a link, or an order, that helped rank the words' popularity: so the most popular term was always used twice as often as the next in line, and three times as often as the one after that.

This relationship, which he called the 'rank vs frequency rule', later known as Zipf's law, was applied to other areas. For example, he went on to show that it could describe income distribution world-wide, with the richest earning double the amount of those next in line. Zipf's law has since proved pertinent to the study of many types of data used in physical and social sciences, even to predicting the size of some of the world's biggest cities.[1]

His work introduced a radical new way to analyse word usage. So, just as in the 1920s avant-garde designers, filmmakers and photographers like Rodchenko, Eisenstein, Vertov and Moholy-Nagy were defamiliarizing our usual way of seeing the world through the use of diagonal framing and unusual perspectives, we can now use software to 'defamiliarize' the way we view visual and media cultures.

Compare this to how art historians through the ages have seemed to spend whole careers studying different parts of paintings created in the Renaissance period and later to determine which bits of the painting belong to studio painters and which to the big-name masters. They were breaking down the complete entity into its component parts to determine provenance. What datafication of culture now offers is the growing ability to use technology to unravel the mysteries of a book, a piece of music or a painting.

An example of this comes from Lev Manovich, founder and director of the US Software Studies Initiative together with Dr Jeremy Douglas and Tara Zepel. They embarked on a quest to compare a million manga images to understand the similarities and differences between the range of graphic techniques used by manga artists (manga refers to comics created in Japan, or by Japanese creators in the Japanese language, stemming from a style developed in Japan in the late 19th century). This type of detailed analysis gives us a chance to delve far more deeply into the artwork as a whole, to see what we might otherwise have missed.[2]

From this we can perhaps start to see an exciting possibility emerging. If we can deconstruct cultural artefacts into their constituent dimensions, then maybe we can start to explore the deeper building blocks of our culture and perhaps identify emerging cultural practices. And because we have an extraordinary library of cultural artefacts all around us we have an incredibly rich 'data set' to work with. This not only includes the books, music and art that we might find in our hallowed libraries, concert halls and galleries but also the explosion in the material that we find across the internet where whole new forms of expression rapidly develop and then fade away again.

Studying popular culture through social media

Popular culture is reflected in social media in a number of ways. Here are a few representative examples.

Text speak. This is used wherever people are online, and employs the abbreviations familiar in all forms of digital communication. The rationale for text speak lies in the origins of mobile telephony. The first mobiles had such a small keypad that users would need to press more than once to input each letter, so abbreviations made life much easier, particularly when they just had 160 characters to play with. And, more importantly, text speak made texting quicker. It proved so popular it began to be used beyond the confines of texting, attracting criticism about its potential impact on literacy. This has lessened with the introduction of alphabetic keyboards on smartphones but nevertheless abbreviations such as LOL (Laugh Out Loud) and PAW (Parents Are Watching) are still frequently used.

Giffing is a prime example of a popular art form that attracted huge amounts of activity and attention but interest in which has since started to fade. It involved users generating a short film, just a few seconds long, before editing it using online tools to give it a jerky, 'cinema reality' look. It was then used to decorate postings and messages with the intent of communicating particular information whether general, maybe about the sender, or with a more specific meaning relating to the message content.

Vine is a Twitter-owned mobile app that offers users the facility to devise and post short looping video clips. Such clips, recorded through the in-app camera, last just six seconds with recording only taking place while the screen is touched. This gives users the opportunity to edit on the move, or create stop/go effects. The resulting video can be shared with Vine's social network and beyond, to say Twitter and Facebook.

Emoji originated in Japan with the use of text patterns to create 'smileys'. These have become hugely more sophisticated with a wide range emoji now in common usage to communicate a range of feelings and information. An interesting discussion has been generated about 'Emoji as Data Culture'.

Of course, social media has attracted much attention from brands as it seems to hold the promise of large-scale access to consumer insight. With 20 per cent of the world's population now having a Facebook account, it is clear that it is an information source that cannot be ignored.

Indeed, there are a wide variety of social media mining companies that brands employ in order to understand the 'sentiment' relating to their brand. This may be very general: are the mentions of our brand overall negative or positive? Alternatively, it may be very specific: how is our latest handset release performing?

Deconstructing cultural trends

But maybe we should set the bar higher in trying to grasp some of the broader themes in our understanding of culture and the underlying context. An example of the possibilities is the 'We Feel Fine' project.[3]

The project is centred on a data collection engine that scans the internet every ten minutes for mentions of 'I feel' or 'I am feeling'. Each mention is scanned to see whether it fits with one of its 5,000 stored 'feelings', a list made up of adjectives and some verbs. If the sentence does, it – and any image found within it – are saved, and deemed to represent that specific 'feeling'. The whole process can result in between 15,000 and 20,000 feelings being saved each day, painting a picture of how many people are feeling 'happy' or 'sad', for example.

This has resulted in a huge database with the potential to reveal how the 'zeitgeist' of how different feelings change over time. The database is searchable by a range of demographics so it is possible to see how the different feelings vary across the population on a global (albeit English-speaking) basis.

The 'We Feel Fine' project does not, however, fundamentally start to apply 'defamiliarization' principles. It continues to engage with the explicit *content* of the message itself rather than understanding its component parts. To explore this we can turn to one of our most important cultural artefacts in history: books. If we want to understand those more embedded, implicit messages within those different cultural artefacts, a good place to start is with the Ngram Viewer[4] (mentioned in Chapter 2).

Sponsored by Google, Erez Aiden and Jean-Baptiste Michel created this graphing application in 2010. Put simply, it records the number of times a word or phrase appears in the 30 million-odd volumes already scanned and digitized by Google. This feeds neatly into a field they also founded: culturomics, in which digitized texts are analysed quantitatively to gain empirical data about human culture.

In their book *Uncharted: Big data as a lens on human culture*,[5] they note that using the Ngram Viewer showed the 10 most common verbs in the English language are irregular, whereas overall most are regular. It also touches on the issue of censorship, running searches on artists branded 'degenerates' by the Nazis and showing via graphs the impact this had on their reputation. Marc Chagall's full name, they say, appears just once in German book records between 1936 and 1943. Another example reveals the spike in mentions of 'Tiananmen' in English-language books post-1989 compared with a momentary rise in Chinese tomes.

Note that this is based on books, so there will be obvious limitations. But it can give useful pointers to the lifecycle of ideas or new concepts. For example, Aiden and Michel charted consistent patterns of debut, growth, peak and slow decline when it comes to celebrities, plus interesting changes over time. Fame is achieved faster now than in the previous century or the one before that, but it fades more quickly too. Meanwhile, their studies show that events such as the sinking of the *Lusitania* in 1915 or the 1972 Watergate scandal followed the same pattern of declining mentions.

Exploring the lifecycle of ideas through cultural analytics

An interesting and relevant example of the way in which this can be applied can be seen with the work undertaken by Alex Bentley and Michael O'Brien, who have explored how Ngram could be used to understand the lifecycle of ideas – in this instance, climate change.[6]

They employed the Ngram database to assess how the popularity of keywords associated with climate change altered over time. As might be expected, they fade year on year. Why is this important to know? Bentley and O'Brien argue that, if scientists wish to influence policy or public opinion, they need to use words that resonate with their target audiences. Scientists leading a more laboratory-focused existence might disagree, as rigorous, specialist-access academic journals seem resistant to the fluctuating popularity of keywords and the blurring of the lines between scientific work and social media.

However, as published materials increasingly compete for attention with digital media, it stands to reason that choice of words becomes more important. In addition, if it is found that keywords associated with a certain science are becoming less popular, it could raise questions about its future. That is why Bentley and O'Brien assert that tools such as Ngram could help maintain research credibility by avoiding the impact of what could be ultimately harmful buzzwords.

Clearly, these findings have got potential relevance for brands. If we can understand the 'half-life' of ideas, interests and what generally occupies our minds (as reflected in the written word), then surely brands can understand when and where to focus their marketing activities. More importantly, we can start to estimate the lifecycle of such ideas: are we at a point where typically we might expect to see the topic remaining in the zeitgeist for several more years or at a point of diminishing returns?

Google's Ngram service has been pretty much ignored by brands up to this point, but surely there could be untapped potential here. For instance, it could track the way in which sales of different product categories or brands relate to key cultural themes. As noted earlier, while it's impossible to isolate causation from this, it does perhaps help us to start formulating hypotheses so that we can start experimenting with ways to capitalize on current dominant cultural themes.

From verbal to visual: the importance of images

Images are increasingly important as 'information vehicles', as it were. We represent ourselves in three key ways: using action, word, and image. Our culture has traditionally focused on the first two and, despite the explosion in the use of images within contemporary culture and society, they have remained an under-explored tool for understanding consumers.

Today, images are the lifeblood of the internet. In its early years, it was of course text-based, used in a functional way to exchange basic, primarily technical, information. As time has gone on, though, the ability to display images has been the primary factor driving internet performance and browser capability. This occurred first on the wild west frontiers of pornography, then with the rich media experiences required by brand-building sites, and now with the prodigious volume of photos and videos shared via social media sites.

It is instructive to recall that 'facebooks' were, and indeed continue to be, US high school photo albums: a reflection of the photo sharing at the heart of social networks. Image-based social networking sites have proliferated with YouTube, Tumblr, Pinterest and Vine all having the explicit function of sharing still or moving images.

Images have always been one of the key building blocks of human culture. They were incredibly important, for example, in cultures like the Roman and Byzantine empires where a lot of citizens couldn't read. Consider all the visual imagery that existed of emperors on coins, and in churches, market places and busy roads. There are plenty of stories of emperors who made themselves look a lot stronger and more handsome in their imagery than they would have been in real life. Their image was official and anyone who tampered with it would get into real trouble.

So while image as a display/creation/support of identity has always been important in the Western world at least, it's the ability of technology to democratize the production and sharing of imagery that has resulted in images playing a new and highly significant role in the formation of identity in contemporary consumer culture.

The sociologist Michel Maffesoli first identified[7] a shift away from traditional forms of identity, arguing that the post-modern era of globalized consumerism weakened the power of nation states to enforce the social institutions of family and class. In a world where the clear social rules and sense of destiny and purpose provided by family and social class were on the wane, he argued that people would seek to form their sense of identity around what he called the 'emotional community'.

This type of identity, formed around a sense of empathy rooted in shared tastes, interests and experiences derived from consumer culture, would lead to the formation of new 'tribes' which would offer people a sense of belonging and containment that the traditional institutions of the family and social class no longer provided so strongly.

This phenomenon, which he first identified in the 1980s, has truly come of age through current social media. Images are now arguably the primary vehicle for the sharing of tastes and experiences that Maffesoli put at the heart of this new way of forming personal and social identities. Compared to language, images offer the global currency necessary for the new tribes that form in social media spaces. They allow quicker and more flexible morphing of meanings and associations, fuelling the sense of novelty, creation and discovery which, as we will see, is essential to creation and expression of identity in social media.

Just as the technological accident of movies starting out as silent (and therefore more culturally universal) allowed for the first era of global media culture, and enabled the explosive growth of the early film industry, so the global currency of images is the main enabler for the latest generation of global media culture – taking into account cultural differences in the understanding of some images, of course.

Take your pick of social networks: they all represent trace signals of the way images are currency in the complex systems of the processes of social identity. This manifests in the flow of images being posted, re-posted and appropriated into entirely new social groups, by different 'tribes'. These images can be seen as a means to capture and entrance – a way of generating 'on the fly' the new sociocultural microspaces which Maffesoli foresaw as the territories of the new tribes. It also explains why there are sites such as Know Your Meme and Urban Dictionary, so that people can educate themselves in whatever is generating the latest buzz in terms of TV shows, films or famous moments in culture and feel part of it.

And, of course, these new social and cultural identities are as likely to be perpetuated by consumers as by brands. When generated by consumers, the images may not be as technically accomplished as those produced by a media agency on behalf of a brand but they will, nevertheless, still include highly sophisticated cues relating to group membership. Images live in the space between brands and consumers, providing the means for the latter to 'consume' the former.

Brands ignore this at their peril: the flow of new forms of social exchange and identity are created and changed at a breakneck pace. It is easy for a brand to misread the ways in which the visual meanings and associations surrounding its imagery can be rapidly and sometimes radically changed, thereby making it essential to be able to read and decode the modern currency of the image.

Attraction of visual marketing

Marketers are seeing the opportunities of visual content, according to online social media magazine *Social Media Examiner*.[8] It reports that, in a study of 3,000 marketers, while some 92 per cent feel that social media is growing in importance as a marketing tool, there is also evidence that more are using – or intend to use – visual content on platforms such as Facebook and Twitter. And there has also been a rise in those using visually-based platforms like Pinterest, YouTube and Instagram.

The research highlights six main findings:

- **Interest in visual marketing rises with experience.** Younger marketers turn to those platforms they are familiar with such as Facebook and Twitter, while those with a track record of five years or more look to more visual platforms (YouTube is fourth most popular with 74 per cent of marketers active on it; followed by Pinterest with 66 per cent and Instagram 47 per cent).

- **Time investment in social media leads to a move to visual platforms.** Two groups of marketers, one devoting 40 hours a week to social media and the other just six, revealed a bias towards visual platforms in the first group.

- **Business-to-consumer (B2C) marketers are more visually focused.** Business-to-business (B2B), by comparison, are fonder of LinkedIn, Google+ and blogging.

- **Visual marketing growth plans.** The report found that 67 per cent of respondents planned to grow their YouTube marketing, and 50 per cent their use of Pinterest.

- **Focus on videos and original visuals**. Some 75 per cent plan to boost their use of original videos, and 70 per cent to increase their use of visual images.

- **Ability to create visual assets is most sought after skill**. Some 68 per cent of marketers ranked it top, followed by training in how to produce original videos (60 per cent).

Analysing cultural trends from images

So just how do we start deriving meaning from the huge amount of images we have available to us, not only those that are user-generated content via social media but also those produced by brands, artists, publishers and so on?

One of the leading researchers in this area is, as mentioned earlier, Dr Lev Manovich. He and his team are using large-scale digitization methods to convert images into their constituent parts so that it is possible to track the way in which the different elements of visuals operate, such as contrast, the presence of texture and fine details, the number of lines and their curvature, the number and type of edges, size and positions of shapes, and so on. Higher order variables (such as what is actually happening in the image) are recorded manually by means of large-scale coding methods using Amazon's Mechanical Turk. This is an online mediated service offered by Amazon which enables individuals and businesses to call on a flexible home-based workforce to perform tasks that computers are currently unable to do.

One way in which he has used this application is with the 'selfie city'.[9] Together with his team he captured 650,000 images that had been downloaded on Instagram over an eight-day period in December 2013 in five cities: Bangkok, Berlin, Moscow, New York and São Paulo. He reduced these down to 640 from each, aiming for a representative sample across categories.

These images were then broken down to identify single person selfies, their age, and gender. Manovich's team's next step was to record whether or not they wore glasses, their mood, the angle of their head and eye position using facial recognition software. This data was then used to highlight any regional or gender trends. Some of the findings were:

- Women in all the cities surveyed proved more enthusiastic about taking photos than men, but once a man hits 30 he is likely to take more selfies than women.

- For some reason, the females of São Paulo adopt a head tilt of 16.9 degrees on average, compared with their peers' 7.6 degrees in New York.

- The people of Moscow don't seem to have a lot to smile about (53 per cent on the smile score scale), but its women take a lot more selfies than men (82 per cent were female generated).

- When the proportion of selfies was compared with the total number of photos culled from social media sites, each city generated an average of just 4 per cent.

- Bangkok has the youngest selfie takers (females 20.3 years old on average, males 22.7) and New York the oldest (women 24.3 and men 26.7), with a median age overall of 23.7.

What Manovich's findings actually mean in the broader scheme of things is less clear. When asked to speculate post-publication, he replied, somewhat enigmatically, 'Your interpretation is as good as mine.' Some observers are filling that 'meaning' gap. For example, in her blog McCrea Davison[10] ventures the suggestion that variations in the number of male and female selfies could be related to the cultural pressure heaped on women to promote their own sexuality and beauty. This could, in turn, impact on the number of selfies posted by women over 30.

Whatever the interpretation, the next phase in the study could prove even more interesting, however. The University of California San Diego is one of six institutions worldwide to have won a Twitter Data Grant for its proposal 'Do happy people take happy images?'[11] The aim of the study, led by Manovich, is to compare the happiness of people in dozens of cities, in effect to take the pulse of society.

So we are starting to see how the deconstruction of images can create a real opportunity for brands to see trends emerging and, as mentioned earlier, fluency in cultural languages can help brands communicate and position themselves in a way that makes full use of this fluency.

Concluding thoughts

There are undoubtedly benefits from understanding visual cultural norms. Brands can ensure that the visual cues they employ are in tune with the zeitgeist. But this still feels as if data is playing too central a role in the process and while patterns are identified we have not got any closer to understanding the forces that shape this data.

Overall, perhaps, this leaves us with a feeling that while there are opportunities in this area there is more work to be done if they are to have practical significance. We have greater possibilities than ever before to convert a range of cultural artefacts into data. And not just on a small scale, as has always been the case, but on an industrial 'big data' scale.

But as the transformation of these artefacts into a data format begins, we need to look (with due care and attention) at their apparent relationship with other attributes, stimulating new hypotheses to be explored. What we have not seen as yet is the marriage of the theoretical foundations of social science theory with the data sets that are increasingly available.

Analysis of the written word has resulted in some interesting modelling of the way in which ideas are adopted and die over time but then it falls short of expectations. We are still left at the point of description rather than developing some broader theoretical principles that allow us to more easily generalize the findings.

Analysis of visual data, meanwhile, has resulted in interesting descriptions of the way in which these have developed but appears to fall short of integrating social science, such as Maffesoli's thinking about tribes, to provide the explanatory principles behind these changes.

Historically we have been limited to analysing cultural artefacts largely at a holistic rather than a 'component' level. Our ability to now do this opens up very interesting new ways by which we can understand the way our culture changes and develops. However, there is a danger of this analysis being undertaken in a very reductive manner, acting as an end in itself rather than contributing to a bigger understanding of how culture and society work. There are huge opportunities here for the ambitious brand strategist who wants, maybe for the first time, to move from a big picture, largely theoretical understanding of the way our culture works to one that is underpinned but also extended by empirical data.

Notes

1 Newitz, Annalee (2013) A mysterious law that predicts the size of the world's biggest cities, *io9* [online] http://io9.com/the-mysterious-law-that-governs-the-size-of-your-city-1479244159

2 Manovich, Lev, Douglass, Jeremy and Zepel, Tara (2013) How to Compare One Million Images? *Software Studies* [online] http://softwarestudies.com/cultural_analytics/2011.How_To_Compare_One_Million_Images.pdf

3 Harris, Jonathan and Kamvar, Sep (2009) *We Feel Fine: An almanac of human emotion*, Scribner Book Company

4 O'Connell, Mark (2014) Bright Lights, Big Data, *The New Yorker* [online] http://www.newyorker.com/online/blogs/books/2014/03/bright-lights-big-data.html

5 Aiden, Erez and Michel, Jean-Baptiste (2013) *Uncharted: Big data as a lens on human culture*, Riverhead Books

6 Bentley, R Alexander and O'Brien, Michael J (2012) The buzzwords of the crowd, *New York Times*, 1 December

7 Maffesoli, Michel (1996) *The Time of the Tribes: The decline of individualism in mass society*, Sage

8 Walter, Ekaterina, Why marketers love Instagram and Pinterest, *Fast Company* [online] http://www.fastcompany.com/3030677/why-seasoned-marketers-are-looking-to-newer-tools-like-instagram-and-pinterest?partner

9   See the Selfie City website at http://selfiecity.net/#intro

10 Davison, McCrea (2014) Response to Lev Manovich's 'Selfie City' Project 11 March [online] http://blogs.cornell.edu/bfamid26/2014/03/11/response-to-lev-manovichs-selfiecity-project/

11 Robbins, Gary (2014) Do happy people take happy photos? *UC San Diego* [online] http://m.utsandiego.com/news/2014/apr/20/twitter-photos-sandiego/

Bright ideas

10

In Chapter 5, 'The power of prediction', we looked at the track record of experts in making judgements about the future. We described a now-famous study by Philip Tetlock, who, in the mid-1980s, began a test that would involve over 280 experts making predictions for the forthcoming 20 years. When he looked at the results two decades later, the results made interesting reading. The experts turned out to be not much better than the control group of undergraduates.

As Tim Harford sets out in his book *Adapt: Why success always starts with failure*:

> The problem is not the experts; it is the world they inhabit – the
> world we all inhabit – which is simply too complicated for anyone to
> analyse with much success.[1]

That sceptical stance seems to have had little impact on the demand for a new breed of expert who make full use of big data: the so-called data scientist. This new breed of guru has become much sought after. As Google's Hal Varian said:

> The sexy job in the next ten years will be statisticians. People think
> I'm joking, but who would've guessed that computer engineering
> would've been the sexy job of the 1990s?[2]

McKinsey, for example, has estimated that in the United States alone there is a shortfall of 140,000 to 190,000 people with analytical expertise and 1.5 million too few managers and analysts with the skills to understand and make decisions based on the analysis of big data.[3]

So what do we need to do?

Indeed, one of the themes of this book is that the world is faced all too often with complex problems. Chapter 5 discussed the key difference between simple systems (where a model can capture all or most of the variation) and complex systems (where there are many interdependent components interacting in non-linear ways) in trying to make sense of what's going on.[4]

Why is it important to understand this distinction? Because much of social and economic activity is complex: it can be almost impossible to capture all the potential variance that needs to be taken into account to make predictions with any degree of confidence. So we need to challenge the notion that a limited number of data scientists are going to provide all the answers from the data an organization has at its disposal.

The point is that the heritage of commercial big data is firmly rooted in highly 'numeric' disciplines including statistics, computer science, applied mathematics, and economics.[5] Where are the social scientists, for example, who can provide much-needed understanding of what to look for in the data, as we have been discussing in the last few chapters? Who will offer a broader perspective and thus extract real value from the data?

Widespread access to data in organizations has been relatively limited for a number of good reasons, including commercial confidentiality and privacy concerns, along with a worry that spreading data too widely can lead to erroneous conclusions. But the downside of this is that too few people – and too few people with the right knowledge and understanding – are making sense of the data. What we now need to consider are models for managing the extraction of value from big data from both within the organization and externally.

Centralization vs decentralization

The way that companies organize and manage data will depend, to a large extent, on their own inherent structure and the framework and guidelines that have evolved for managing business operations. One of the constant themes of management literature over the years has been the benefits of centralized vs decentralized decision-making.

For many brands a centralized structure helps maintain control over a vast international operation, and ensures consistency of customer experience. Others, meanwhile, may give managers at a local level a certain amount of decision-making power when it comes to staffing, sales promotion or customer-facing queries. Whatever option organizations choose, the challenge is to harness and deal creatively with data while growing the level of expert participation.

It's safe to say that organizations that cast their net wide when looking at data are likely acting sensibly. But rather than casting it wide and then adopting a centralized approach, allowing local teams greater access might arguably produce better results. It is a constant debate, as all large organizations wrestle with how best to manage and exploit the growing avalanche of data.

Economist and philosopher Friedrich Hayek took the view that organizations should consider the purpose of the information itself. Centralized decision-making can be more cost-effective and co-ordinated, he believed, but decentralization can add speed and local information that proves more valuable, even if the bigger picture is less clear.

He argued that organizations thought too highly of centralized knowledge, while ignoring 'knowledge of the particular circumstances of time and place'. But it is relatively recently that economists are starting to accumulate data that allows them to gauge how successful organizations manage themselves.[6]

One such exercise described by Tim Harford was carried out by Harvard Professor Julie Wulf and the former chief economist of the International Monetary Fund, Raghuram Rajan.[7] They reviewed the workings of large US organizations over fifteen years from the mid-1980s. What they found was a move towards decentralization, often driven by globalization and the need to react promptly to a diverse and swift-moving range of markets, particularly at a local level. These companies found that decentralization pays.

Interestingly, it would be logical to expect that increasingly sophisticated information technology and better communication links would enhance the appeal of centralization, making it easier for a planner to locate all the data needed in one spot and thus make key decisions. Yet it appears that technological advancement often goes hand-in-hand with decentralization. It offers speed and flexibility, but getting the most out of it requires a skilled, adaptable workforce that have been given the freedom to make their own decisions.

This shift is being accelerated by the way that data is used throughout organizations. Data analytics is filtering down to the department layer, where executives are eager to trawl through the mass of information on offer. Cloud computing, meanwhile, means that line managers no longer rely on IT teams to deploy computer resources. They can do it themselves, in just minutes.[8]

The decentralization trend is also impacting on technology spending. According to Gartner,[9] chief marketing officers have been given the same purchasing power in this area as IT managers and, as their spending rises, so that of data centre managers is falling.

Tim Harford makes a strong case for the way in which this decentralization is important given that the environment in which we operate is so unpredictable (as we discussed in Chapter 5). Innovation typically comes, he argues, from a 'swirling mix of ideas, not from isolated minds'. And Jane Jacobs, writer on urban planning observed that we should look for innovation in cities rather than on the Pacific Islands.[10]

Looking beyond the data

We first referred to Donald Marchand and Joe Peppard's work in Chapter 3.[11] In the course of a study of over 50 international companies across a range of industries they discovered the tendency of organizations to approach projects using the huge amounts of data now available in the same way they would approach existing IT projects: using IT specialists with a focus on building and deploying technology on time, to plan, and within budget.

Yet this is to ignore the valuable insights that could be available if time were taken to approach it with an understanding of just how people create and use information. It calls for the inclusion of other types of experts as well. The authors have drawn up five guidelines for companies wishing to gain the most from big data projects:

- put users – those who will create meaning from the information – at the heart of the initiative;

- unlock value from IT by asking second-order questions and giving teams the freedom to reframe business problems;

- equip teams with cognitive and behavioural scientists, who understand how people perceive problems and analyse data;

- focus on learning by facilitating information sharing, examining assumptions, and striving to understand cause and effect;

- worry more about solving business problems than about deploying technology.

Developing organization-wide networks of experts

One approach to gaining access to more expertise is to build communities of experts rather than going outside the organizational walls.

In 2001 IBM, for example, launched what it called 'jams' to encourage its 400,000 employees to apply their thinking to the type of strategic questions that were normally the preserve of IBM high flyers or top consultants.[12] They managed this by a variety of means, from emails to wikis to collaborative projects. The scheme delivered results: in 2003 the network helped with the revision of IBM's core values statement, and then three years later – via an 'innovation jam' – it produced a host of big new ideas, five of which have become key to its 'smarter planet' initiative.

The 'jam' concept exploited the fact that more and more IBM employees were either working from home or at client sites. The sheer speed of a jam – interlinking bulletin boards and related web pages on the company's intranet but managed centrally – meant staff felt involved and listened to, while making a valuable contribution to IBM in terms of new ideas. As a motivational tool, it has the ability to engage tens of thousands of people simultaneously.[13]

The power of jamming

There is growing interest in the idea of 'jamming' as part of the innovation process. Yet it is deceptively complex and can be hard to get right. Alessandro Di Fiore compiled his own 'how to' guide[14] following work at the European Centre for Strategic Innovation, comparing how different companies structured and ran jamming sessions. The most successful shared certain common practices.

1. Keep it simple and small scale

The Centre discovered that participants who chose their own challenge or problem were far more committed – and creative – than those who were assigned one. Smaller teams allow members to get to know each other and their ways of working more effectively than bigger ones, with four in each team allowing sufficient diversity and engagement for a swift response to the challenges selected.

2. Take time to define

Confused thinking, or a desire to get the 'jamming' process rolling, can mean teams are given problem statements that are too broad or ill-defined, often ambiguous or laden with jargon, so that they struggle to engage with them. Di Fiore recommends investing in the necessary time upfront, so that the problem is defined succinctly.

3. Training is key

Jamming, like any form of exercise, is improved by practice. This relates not just to the act of problem definition and brainstorming, but also to the need to spend time engaging with creative thinking tools that can be used in the ideation processes. Di Fiore also found that training in the use of strategic innovation frameworks would improve the business relevance of team outputs.

4. Fun fuels effectiveness

Jamming should be a fun process, because fun and creativity go hand in hand. So factor in time for play, because this needs practice, too. He recommends bringing in a conjuror or clown to help break the ice. The role of the facilitator as master of ceremonies will be a tricky one: they need to keep the atmosphere light, but also know when to return to the business in hand.

Using external networks

Increasingly organizations consider there are benefits to be gained from opening up access to a wider circle of individuals in the search for innovative ideas. Two of these are explored below.

Crowdsourcing expertise

Traditionally, knowledge has for centuries been in the hands of the few, argues David Weinberger, senior researcher at Harvard's Berkman Center for Internet & Society, co-director of Harvard's Library Innovation Lab, and co-author of the best-seller *The Cluetrain Manifesto*. In his latest book[15] the philosopher/marketing guru observes how experts have been clustered in various types of networks since ancient Greece, mainly because of physical constraints (in other words, the limits on the means of communication). This meant it made sense to assemble only those who had the right knowledge.

But the advent of the internet changed that constraint, he argues. The term 'crowdsourcing' was first used by Jeff Howe in a 2006 article for *Wired*. It means that now you can have any number of people examining and commenting on data. Weinberger mentions the site set up by the UK newspaper *The Guardian* to get readers to examine 700,000 expenses claims from Members of Parliament to look for frivolous deductions. Some 20,000 people flocked to help.

How does that apply to business, however, where the emphasis is so often on confidentiality? The wider you cast the net, the more likely it is you will find people who have the skills and understanding you require.

One example, again cited by Weinberger, is that of Primary Insight, a consultancy set up to offer clients expertise from a network of thousands of part-time experts, who are nonetheless leaders in their fields. The business claims that its very variety is its strength, since expertise is not limited to a few full-time specialists who can be used as necessary.

Consumer goods specialist Procter & Gamble (P&G) has eagerly embraced the idea of crowdsourcing in the search for sustainable innovation. Not only is it recognized for innovation in consumer-learning tools, the company also gains insights from crowdsourcing via digital platforms such as Vocalpoint to connect with an 'army of moms' (Vocalpoint has 250,000 members) for insights on products like Dawn, Febreze and Millstone coffee, as well as a 'virtual world store' that simulates a retail environment to test consumer reaction to promotions and layouts.[16]

Contests

Another approach Weinberger discusses is the contest. Unlike crowd-sourcing, however, this has a long and varied history. In the early 18th century, for example, the British parliament offered £20,000 to anyone who could solve the problem of determining longitude at sea.

It was the origin of the modern Longitude Prize, a contest built on a £10 million prize fund to solve some of the world's pressing issues. In 2014, for example, the British public voted for the prize to be awarded to antibiotics, which was up against projects in six critical areas such as water and food. Competitors from across the globe have up to five years to put their solution forward for assessment.

Spreading the net so much wider in this way ensures that potential solutions have a much better chance of emerging and is the principle behind MIT's Climate CoLab, a collaborative online community centred around a series of annual contests that seek out promising ideas for fighting climate change.[17]

Wikipedia was arguably one of the pioneers in encouraging the general population to generate ideas, gather information, and solve sticky problems, as with many open source software projects. According to Christian Terwiesch, professor of operations and information management at the Wharton School at the University of Pennsylvania,[18] having more people working on a challenge translates into more ideas, better ideas, and more diverse ideas that can then be filtered down. Adding a contest element gives the crowdsourcing process a level of legitimacy and helps motivate potential contributors.

Another example comes from Weinberger. In 2009 the Sunlight Foundation, a non-partisan organization dedicated to promoting more government transparency, ran the 'Apps for America' contest to encourage people to come up with ways to extract value from the avalanche of data being made public by the federal government. Run again the following year, it resulted in a prize of US $15,000 for the winner.

A number of companies now operate as contest-based expertise brokers. For example, InnoCentive, set up in 2001, has been involved in solutions to many thousands of challenges, such as:

- Partnering with Prize4Life in 2006 to launch the $1 million ALS Biomarker Prize with the goal of accelerating the development of a biomarker – an inexpensive and easy-to-use tool that can accurately measure the progression of ALS (also known as Lou Gehrig's disease and motor neurone disease) in patients. An effective biomarker will make clinical trials of ALS drugs cheaper, quicker, and more efficient. The prize was awarded in 2011 to a neurologist for his identification of a biomarker which marks a significant step forward in ALS research.

- In the summer of 2007, the Oil Spill Recovery Institute (OSRI) posted three challenges, all dealing with recovery issues. The first was solved by someone whose expertise was in the concrete industry, not oil.

- Many problems afflict developing countries, such as poverty, women's safety, literacy and disease: add to the list the lack of electricity. SunNight Solar wanted to develop a dual-purpose solar light that would function as a lamp and a flashlight to be used in African villages and other areas of the world without electricity. To find a solution, it turned to the InnoCentive Solver community. An electrical engineer from New Zealand solved the challenge and was awarded $20,000 in March 2008, two months after the Challenge was posted.

Limitations to using networks

There is an argument that some of the attempts at generating alternative views of the data are simplistic because the expectations of what can be achieved in a 48-hour hackathon competition with beer and pizza may be unduly high. And because the fact that this may have worked in the technology sector often seems to imbue these approaches with a magical quality which could be dangerously misleading when it comes to solving business issues.

Evgeny Morozov[19] warns against this growing tendency, arguing that technology is increasingly encouraging 'solutionism thinking'. He describes this as recasting all complex social situations either as neat problems with definite, computable solutions or as transparent and self-evident processes that can be easily optimized – if only the right algorithms are in place.

His concerns are aimed at the way this is applied in government and the public sector, where he considers 'sexy, monumental, and narrow-minded solutions' are applied to 'problems that are extremely complex, fluid, and contentious'. How, he asks, will such 'solutionism' affect our society, once deeply political, moral, and irresolvable dilemmas are recast as uncontroversial and easily manageable matters of technological efficiency? The very same question can be asked of this approach for brands of course.

Another challenge is managing data privacy when engaging with an extended network. It can sound very enticing to extend the network of people involved in finding answers to technological issues, but to what extent can that be applied to business? How far can a brand owner go, for instance, in releasing confidential information on such a widespread and public scale?

The now-infamous example is when Netflix, the internet subscription service, set up the highly-publicized Netflix Prize in 2006. It was an open competition for the best collaborative filtering algorithm to predict user ratings for films, based on previous ratings and without any other information about the users or films, ie without the users or the films being identified except by numbers assigned for the contest.

The problems came when some researchers found that they could identify actual users by overlaying other behavioural and demographic databases.[20] This re-identification potential led to the prize being cancelled in early 2010.

Nurturing ideas

Tim Harford, whose book, *Adapt*, we mentioned earlier, sets out a very convincing case for trial and error as a sensible strategy for businesses. His discussion of Skunk Works is relevant in this context of this chapter. Here is almost the converse of spreading the net wide – skunk works is the practice of allowing a small and probably unconventional team to exist within a large organization who are deliberately protected from a twitchy corporate machine. The classic example here is of the aero engineering company Lockheed Martin, whose Skunk Works team designed a number of highly successful new aeroplanes. He makes the point that this model won't guarantee success but if the occasional one does occur then it may well be worth the investment.

And many brands have adopted just such an approach, from defence supplier Raytheon's 'Bike Shop', Amazon's secretive 'Lab126' through to Google's 'Google X' lab.[21] The point that Harford makes is that brands see the value in these teams because it is recognized that we are in a constantly changing environment where new ideas need room to breathe. Given that predictions are hard to make with real certainty, then an evolutionary mix of small initiatives and the odd reckless gamble is probably the best way to look for solutions.

The point is that these kind of skunk works give breathing space to ideas, allowing them to run in parallel. A little like Zara's approach to retailing we discussed in Chapter 5, we can then see which of these fall on stony ground and which others find fertile soil and take root. As Harford puts it, 'In an uncertain world, we need more than just Plan A; and that means finding safe havens for Plans B, C, D and beyond.'

Concluding thoughts

One of the challenges that brands have is to balance the benefits that come with a decentralized approach to data access with the downsides – notably privacy and security. Nevertheless, some mid-point needs to be found because, as this book has made consistently plain, data analytics cannot exist in a vacuum. As technology costs plummet then it is ever easier to facilitate access to data and also to provide platforms that have some inherent guidance embedded within them – so issuing warnings if the number of cases falls too low for reliable conclusions to be drawn.

To some extent brands do not really have a choice. Relationships with consumers are increasingly data-mediated and as such many more people throughout the organization will need access to systems that allow them both to manage these relationships but also to better understand and analyse them at the same time.

The big opportunity is for brands to start introducing a wider range of data analysts into their teams beyond the usual economists, mathematicians and computer scientists. More can be done to include social scientists – psychologists, sociologists, geographers – and in doing so develop links with academic institutions. There is potential for real value exchange here as academics are often starved of data to explore and frankly businesses often need new ideas to unravel longstanding knotty issues.

Despite the potential pitfalls of casting the net wider for data analytics, there are huge benefits to be had. In a sense this book has been all about the way in which a wider community needs to be involved in big data. Brands that hope to gain differentiation through their big data investments may find that this is rapidly eroded if it is purely a technology solution rather than one which has broad intellectual input from a stakeholder population that understands both the business issues and the consumer perspective.

Notes

1 Harford, Tim (2011) *Adapt: Why success always starts with failure*, Hachette

2 Hal Varian on how the Web challenges managers, *McKinsey Quarterly*, January 2009 [online] http://www.mckinsey.com/insights/innovation/hal_varian_on_how_the_web_challenges_managers

3 Manyika, J, Chui, M, Brown, B, Bughin, J, Dobbs, R, Roxburgh, C and Byers, A (2011) Big data: the next frontier for innovation, competition and productivity, *McKinsey Global Institute*, May

4 Watts, Duncan J (2011) *Everything is Obvious Once You Know the Answer: How common sense fails*, Atlantic Books

5 McKinsey & Company (2012) *Big data: the next frontier for innovation, competition, and productivity*, McKinsey Global Institute

6 Harford, Tim (2011) (see note 1 above)

7 Rajan, Raghuram G and Wulf, Julie (2006) Are perks purely managerial excess? *Journal of Financial Economics*, Elsevier, 79 (1), pp 1–33, January

8 Korzeniowski, Paul (2013) Following both sides of the decentralized vs centralized IT debate, *TechTarget* [online] *http://searchdatacenter. techtarget.com/opinion/Following-both-sides-of-the-decentralized-vs-centralized-IT-debate*

9 By 2017 the CMO will spend more on IT than the CIO (webinar) *Gartner* 3 January 2012 [online] http://my.gartner.com/portal/server.pt ?open=512&objID=202&mode=2&PageID=5553&resId=1871515&r ef=Webinar-Calendar

10 Jacobs, Jane (1993) *The Death and Life of Great American Cities*, Random House Modern Library

11 Marchand, Donald and Peppard, Joe (2013) Why IT fumbles analytics, *Harvard Business Review*, January

12 See the IBM Jam events page at https://www.collaborationjam.com/

13 Bjelland, Osvald M and Chapman Wood, Robert (2008) An inside view of IBM's innovation jam, *MIT Sloan Management Review*, 1 October

14 Di Fiore, Alessandro (2013) Making your next innovation jam work, *Harvard Business Review*, 18 January

15 Weinberger, David (2012) *Too Big to Know: Rethinking knowledge now that the facts aren't the facts, experts are everywhere, and the smartest person in the room is the room*, Basic Books

16 de Jong, Marc, Marston, Nathan, Roth, Erik and van Biljon, Peet (2013) The eight essentials of innovation performance, *McKinsey Quarterly*, December

17 See the climatecolab website at www.climatecolab.org

18 Shemkus, Sarah (2014) Crowdsourcing climate change, one contest at a time, *The Guardian*, 15 April

19 Morozov, Evgeny (2014) *To Save Everything, Click Here: The folly of technological solutionism*, Public Affairs

20 Narayanan, Arvind and Shmatikov, Vitalym (2008) Robust de-anonymization of large datasets. In *Proceedings of the 2008 IEEE Symposium on Security and Privacy*, pp 111–125 [online] http://arxiv. org/PS_cache/cs/pdf/0610/0610105v2.pdf

21 Nisen, Max (2013) 17 of the most mysterious corporate labs, *Business Insider* [online] http://www.businessinsider.com/coolest-skunk-works-2013–2?op=1

PART THREE
Consumer thinking

Off limits?

11

As discussed in Chapter 1, data has become the fuel that powers so many aspects of our lives. In many such data-intensive sectors as finance, healthcare and e-commerce there is a huge amount of data available on individual behaviours and outcomes. But there is also a growing 'datafication' of traditionally non-digital parts of our lives.

But consumers and the public in general are beginning to express real concern over the way data is handled. In a 2013 Gfk/*Guardian* poll,[1] 69 per cent of UK consumers claimed they found the way that brands handled their personal data to be 'creepy'. The vast majority said they would be more likely to give their business to a brand that 'respects my privacy'. We have seen large numbers of consumers download ad-blocking software so that over one in five visitors to websites now have some form of ad blocking in place.[2] And companies are springing up to offer privacy services such as Snapchat, where images are only available for a short amount of time, through to Blackphone, a mobile phone providing encryption for phone calls, emails, texts, and internet browsing.

Why have these concerns begun to emerge? It's hard to believe that after years of handing over huge amounts of personal data to a wide range of online brands that people have suddenly become bashful. Or could it be that the public has suddenly become more conscious of how its data is being used and is increasingly sceptical of assurances by both governments and brands that there are mechanisms in place to ensure that personal data will be used carefully and responsibly?

This chapter will highlight the limits to personalization in the brand/consumer relationship and how the growth of consumer tracking techniques can actually harm those relationships by changing consumer behaviour.

How people think about data sharing

It's probably fair to say that until relatively recently few people had thought much about their personal data. After all, it is a fairly vague concept and, as the psychology literature makes plain, people tend to focus on what's clear and visible rather than abstract and vague.[3] So much of the time it's simply something that people don't think about.

However, this is changing. The revelations from former US intelligence analyst Edward Snowden about the way in which security services were accessing and using personal data seem to have been one of the key turning points. Meanwhile, in the UK the media has covered a range of topics on the use and misuse of personal data, from litter bins embedded with wi-fi sniffing software[4] through to the amassing of health records by the UK government's Care.data programme.[5]

Behavioural economics, or the psychology of the economic decision-making of individuals, can help us understand why this is happening. The first step is to understand the difference between a market relationship and a social relationship. As Dan Ariely, a leading behavioural economist, puts it, after a meal at your in-laws for Thanksgiving in the United States you would not pull your wallet out and ask what payment you could offer for the meal. That's because this is the warm and fuzzy world of *social* relationships where a price is not put on something (unlike in a *market* relationship). There is a sense of natural trust and no need for immediate reciprocity.[6]

Conversely, when going out to eat at a restaurant, you don't lean back in your chair at the end of the meal, thank the waiter kindly and leave without paying. It is understood that in a market relationship a price has been set which needs to be honoured.

The problem for organizations collecting and handling personal data is that, when leveraging value from it, these social and market norms can collide. For example, people generally understand that there are definite social norms implicit in their relationships with public institutions, which include a shared understanding of civic rights and responsibilities. Most of our public and private institutions rely on the 'good will' of social norms. So not only will the general public feel angry when these are violated but their behaviour may well change in ways that create more trouble and expense in the long run.

One of the challenges facing organizations handling personal data is that when leveraging value from the data they have collected, these social and market norms can collide. There are certainly social norms implicit in our relationships with our public institutions, with a shared understanding of our civic rights and responsibilities. So, I share all manner of information about myself with my doctor and whilst I may expect this to be used for the good of others (social norms) I don't necessarily expect it to be sold to insurance companies (market norms). Similarly I may share information about myself that makes it easier for brands to do business with me (social norms) but I may then not expect them to use it for targeted advertising (market norms). So brands need to be mindful of the context in which data will have been shared, as there are implicit assumptions about reasonable use and fairness that underpin the way in which consumers share their data.

Another lesson from psychology on the effect of data-mediated relationships is the 'endowment effect'.[7] This is a phenomenon whereby people tend to place greater value on what they own. Privacy researcher Alessandro Acquisti found just such an effect[8] in relation to personal data. In a study he ran, people who started an experiment from positions of greater privacy protection were found to be five times more likely than other people (who did not start with that protection) to forgo money to preserve their privacy. When personal data is discussed in the media or in government-led public consultation processes around data-related issues, it tends to be emphasized that it is 'your data'. Note that the UK government's Care.data leaflet emphasizes that it is 'your health records' and 'your information' that is being requested. Emphasizing this ownership presses the endowment effect button whereby the public will place greater value on the data and therefore have heightened sensitivity about the way in which it is then used.

Limits to data-mediated relationships

Marketers have enthusiastically adopted the mantra that personalized marketing is the right strategy for their brand. And, while much of the time this may well have a lot to recommend it, there is currently very little understanding of the optimal way it should be deployed.

Any discomfort on the part of consumers is often explained as merely the symptoms of a mindset that is taking time to adjust to new forms of advertising. After all, few consumers claim to love television advertising yet there is plenty of evidence to show that they both accept it and are influenced by it. Brands, however, should bear in mind that there is a growing debate about the possibility of getting trapped into the 'uncanny valley' where consumers reject highly-personalized marketing approaches.

The term uncanny valley was first used in 1970 by Japanese roboticist Masahiro Mori[9] who noted that, although we tend to warm to robots that have some human features, we feel uncomfortable when they start becoming too realistic. And while there has been little empirical evidence to support this claim, it has nevertheless been gaining momentum steadily ever since.

The uncanny valley effect has since been blamed[10] for the failure of a number of films that used CGI to produce very human-like characters but where the audience is aware that they are, in fact, animations. The film *Polar Express* is often cited as an example where the effects left it with lacklustre box office sales whereas films such as *Brave* or *The Incredibles* used characters that were clearly not human and fared much better.

Research undertaken by the author and fellow researchers Dr Guy Champniss and Dr Kiki Koutmeridou has identified an uncanny valley phenomenon in relation to marketing communications. Initially, consumers enjoy the personalization of marketing communications, with steadily improving brand attachment as personalization increases. However, there then appears to be a line that is crossed when there is too much personalization for consumers' comfort and brand attachment rapidly declines, falling into an 'uncanny valley'.

Our research, as shown in Figure 11.1, certainly suggests that this is the case – albeit with a little variance early on in the data.

Of course, where brands tip over into an uncanny valley may well depend on a variety of factors. Some categories may be more

FIGURE 11.1 Impact of increased personalization on brand attachment

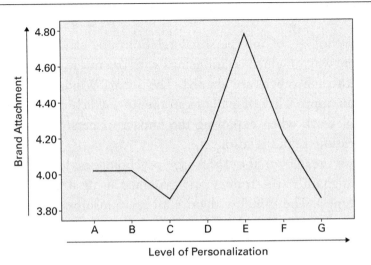

associated with hyper-personalization and therefore more accepted. What is considered appropriate for Google may not be right for a consumer goods brand. We also find very clear differences in receptiveness to targeted advertising across different population segments – partly, but not wholly, based on demographics such as age, gender and lifestyle.

Marketers need to start asking where the uncanny valley might begin for their brand, because the brand's marketing activity might just be doing the opposite of what is intended and actually turning consumers off. Similarly, governmental schemes to improve citizens' lives may not be adopted as enthusiastically as hoped due to this phenomenon.

A possible example of the uncanny valley in action comes from Qantas.[11] Flight attendants now have very detailed data on the airline's highly valued frequent flyers displayed on their onboard tablets. Despite this being something actually sought by Qantas staff, they found it difficult to incorporate this information into their interactions in a way that felt natural. So instead of making their most valued customers feel looked after, this data-driven approach too often 'creeped them out'.

A model for thinking about data-mediated relationships

The psychology of interpersonal relationships can help us understand the way in which relationships with organizations (rather than just with each other) are shaped. The Johari Window is an example of an approach, originally from therapy, which can act as a useful framework when exploring the impact of personal data on the organization–brand relationship.

It was created in the 1950s by psychologists Joseph Luft and Harry Ingham[12] (the framework is named using a combination of their names). The Window divides all relationships into four areas, determined by whether the information is known to the individual or the world, or for our purposes, to the individual or the organization:

- Open Self: This is where the information is shared by both the individual and the organization. So my shopping behaviour with my supermarket falls into this category, since we both share the same knowledge about it.

- Hidden Self: This is information that I know about myself but my supermarket does not know. This would include my shopping activity at other supermarkets but also major life events, my desires and aspirations.

- Blind Self: This is where the supermarket knows things about me that I don't know about myself. This might include my profitability to the organization, the degree to which I have optimized my shopping activity, where I sit in their segmentation and how the organization intends to engage with me.

- Unknown Self: This is where information about me sits that neither the supermarket nor I know. I may have unconscious needs and desires that are not yet revealed even to myself, let alone my supermarket.

How can this model help us to understand the way in which personal data can influence relationships? As organizations collect more information about us from a variety of sources, then the amount about me that is unknown to my supermarket starts to shrink. My Hidden Self starts to shrink as my activity with other brands is increasingly available to organizations through sharing or selling consumers' personal data.

These shifts in the known versus unknown selves can create an imbalance in the relationship with organizations which can be uncomfortable for the individual who is concerned about the amount and type of information held on them. As such the risk for organizations is that the public starts to withdraw from the relationship. The GfK/*Guardian* study found, for example, that 83 per cent of UK consumers are more likely to give their business to companies that they trust will use their information appropriately.

People can also be uncomfortable when shown their 'Blind Self'. An article by Sara Watson for *The Atlantic* magazine[13] described the way in which online advertising can at times be so unnerving:

> When our data doesn't match our understanding of ourselves, the uncanny emerges... With digital traces assembled by personalization engines, our most intimate behaviours are uncovered and reflected back to us. We don't think an ad is relevant to us, but it repulses us because we are worried that it could be.

But the individual has no real way of knowing whether this is based on information that is specific to them or encompasses a much wider category of individuals. As Watson points out, 'We don't often get to ask our machines, "What makes you think that about me?"'

So, like it or not, people are pushed into this situation where inferences that are made about them are reflected back to them. But understanding how they are being categorized by organizations can make people feel less individual. This is certainly consistent with another facet of the uncanny valley study, which measured the creativity of those who had been exposed to different levels of personalization.

This used the classic test of asking for the number of uses of a brick. We found that those exposed to higher personalization scenarios exhibited significantly less creative responses to this question than those tested with the low personalization scenario. Arguably, this can be considered a reflection of the way in which greater personalization demonstrates to each of us that our actions, rather than being a reflection of what we like to consider as our multi-faceted unique selves, are in fact routinely predictable. As such this can make us feel less individual.

Overstepping data-based relationships

Studying the brand/consumer relationship through the prism of the Johari Window can thus offer valuable insights for brands into the limits of personalization. There is, however, a deeper question to consider: given that consumers are increasingly at a point where they have an awareness of the way in which brands are tracking their behaviour, does this 'surveillance' in itself have an impact on them and, if so, can it be understood?

Chris Chambers, senior research fellow in cognitive neuroscience at Cardiff University recently summarized the literature[14] as it related to government surveillance of its citizens. One of the key findings is that surveillance leads to heightened levels of stress, fatigue and anxiety.[15] Further, we know that surveillance encourages conformity to social norms,[16] consistent with the uncanny valley research on creativity, discussed in the previous section.

Does it matter to brands if their collective tracking activity leads to heightened stress, fatigue and anxiety or indeed encourages conformity to social norms? As long as purchases are being made and there has been a sufficient duty of care being demonstrated by the brand then surely there is no real commercial case to be made to do otherwise?

But if the very act of tracking consumer behaviour can have longer-term commercial implications for the brand, that would be short-sighted. To explore this it's useful to understand the different sorts of relationships that may exist between brands and consumers and the possible effect of behavioural tracking on these relationships. Just as a therapist seeks a better understanding of their client in the therapy room, so a brand is collecting data to better understand the consumer.

The philosopher Martin Buber[17] considered that there were three broad types (perhaps levels) of relating:

- 'I–Thou', where people treat others as equals in every way – so all of their well-being is at least as important as our own;

- 'I–You', where we don't really consider others as properly equal but do recognize others' rights and feelings;

- 'I–It', where others are considered purely as objects and treated accordingly.

The importance of relationships for brands has long been underestimated, according Jill Avery, Susan Fournier and John Wittenbraker in a recent HBR article.[18] They argue that 'despite the "R" in CRM and US $11 billion spent on CRM software annually, many companies don't understand customer relationships at all.' They believe that brands lack 'relational intelligence'. By this they mean that there is a lack of awareness of the range of relationships customers can have with an organization or indeed how to operate between different types of relationship.

They examine the breadth of relationships that exist and how companies can improve their bottom line by getting better at capturing data that tells which, of a broad range of relational types, their customers are looking for. While some customer/brand relationships can operate quite happily in a fairly transactional manner (such as 'complete strangers' or 'fleeting acquaintances') there is an acknowledgement that market share accrues to a more in-depth relationship (such as 'best friends' or 'marriage partners').

We can broadly transpose this with our different levels of relating where 'I–It' is more transactional and 'I–Thou' is where many higher-end brands in engaged categories aspire to be: a 'loved' brand. But what if data-mediated relationships inadvertently encourage an 'I–It' model generally, where individuals are looking at relationships to reinforce a particular image of themselves rather than to engage more actively?

Many commentators certainly consider that technology may be encouraging this mode of communication with each other. As Sherry Turkle puts it in her book, *Alone Together*:[19]

> We use social networking to be 'ourselves,' but our online performances take on lives of their own. Our online selves develop distinct personalities. Sometimes we see them as our 'better selves.' As we invest in them, we want to take credit for them.

She cites a case study, 'Brad' to illustrate the effect of this:

> To me, the smoke signals suggest a kind of reduction and betrayal. Social media ask us to represent ourselves in simplified ways. And then, faced with an audience, we feel pressure to conform to these simplifications. On Facebook, Brad represents himself as cool and in the

know – both qualities are certainly part of who he is. But he hesitates to show people online other parts of himself (like how much he likes Harry Potter). He spends more and more time perfecting his online Mr Cool. And he feels pressure to perform him all the time because that is who he is on Facebook.

For brands, the danger is that as people grow more aware that their behaviour is subject to ever-closer scrutiny, they start to conform to what is expected of them in that relationship. Writer Bryan Appleyard talks about this with reference to call trees.[20]

> This is a future that both humans and machines are building and the process demonstrates the difficulties involved in constructing that future without reconstructing humans. Call trees are a way of simplifying human callers so that they can be understood by the machine. The options queues do not offer routes to all the answers you might want, but only to those the machine can provide.

And indeed Nicholas Carr wrote on similar themes when he famously asked in The *Atlantic* magazine, 'Is Google making us stupid?'.[21] There is a danger that technology not only shifts people's relationships between themselves to more of an 'I–It' relationship but also, perhaps, that they increasingly become the 'It' in their relationship with technology. As brands collect more and more information about individuals they become a 'known quantity', where the brand has a spreadsheet in hand calculating which strategies will result in the desired response.

So while brands may typically aspire to have an 'I–Thou' relationship with their customers, perhaps the imbalance that people perceive as the Unknown Self declines makes this harder. More significantly, there is a danger that individuals are being trained to engage with brands in a way that flattens their responses and reflects their idealized selves rather than their true selves.

The purpose of this is not to suggest that data-mediated relationships can never be successful. There are, of course, plenty of well-documented examples where brands have used digital consumer engagement to real advantage. But we should question whether the relationship is a purely linear one and what the implications are for the broader, strategic brand health in the longer term.

Looking beyond the data

Can personal data be used instead for forming the basis of healthy long-term relationships? There is a sense that the changing information flows that technology allows could indeed facilitate this for brands, producing an opportunity for much more dialogue and interaction.

But is an 'I–Thou' or even 'I–You' relationship possible when you have one party holding most of the cards? Where, for instance, if the Johari Window balance has tipped in favour of the Blind Self, the supermarket is in danger of knowing more about someone than they know about themselves? Perhaps this is why the story about US supermarket Target has become such a talisman for the power of Big Data. Charles Duhigg relayed[22] how Target identified a teenager as pregnant based on her shopping habits, resulting in mailings to her house. Her enraged father complained to Target about these inappropriate mailings only to call back later to apologize when sure enough he found out she was indeed pregnant.

Are there ways to address this imbalance? Brands could, for example, help consumers to reduce their Blind Self. Better sharing of the information held by brands could help those individuals know themselves better. For example, did you know that your grocery buying pattern potentially puts you at high risk of heart disease? That your banking behaviours reveal particular attitudes towards risk? Of course, if it is not positioned in the right way to consumers with appropriate levels of permissions sought and opt-out available then there is the potential that this can be seen as invasive and creepy by consumers. But if consumers benefit from such insights and experience personal growth they might feel less uncomfortable about the data held about them. Interestingly, many governments worldwide are launching programmes that will require brands to make personal data held about consumers available to them. This creates the opportunity for brands to position themselves as 'decision support services', which may well be a valuable opportunity for brands to better engage with their customer base.[23]

The Unknown Self is also an interesting area where there ought to be opportunities for growth for both parties. As data analysis techniques improve, brands can start to find out ever-more sophisticated insights about us that we didn't know ourselves. If the Unknown Self is explored in a collaborative manner then we may well appreciate the insight and our relationship may strengthen and grow as a result. Of course the above caveats about appropriate consent and opt-outs apply more than ever.

Concluding thoughts

There is plenty of evidence that the increased availability of data can have a huge impact for brands, reducing costs, enhancing efficiency and generating a much greater understanding of their customers. And there is little doubt that there are real business benefits with plenty of success stories to illustrate the way in which brands can use personal data to good effect.

But the discussion to date has been a little lopsided. Much of the debate has implicitly assumed a linear relationship between the increased use of personal data and business growth. What this chapter asks is whether the relationship is in fact not as simple as this. There are psychological, social and cultural factors that suggest the relationship is not straightforward. A very clear demonstration of this is the research showing an 'uncanny valley' that can open up in brand attachment as personalization increases. This certainly suggests that the relationship between personal data usage and brand attachment is one that may be far from linear.

Perhaps it is tempting to think of these issues as noise around the fringes which will disappear as cultural norms gradually become more accepting of different methods of engagement between consumers and brands. But this seems too simplistic an interpretation. Personal data fundamentally changes the dynamics of the relationship in ways that are hard to predict. Brands now know very intimate details about consumers that they themselves may have no awareness of. We simply don't yet properly understand how this impacts the nature of the relationship between brands and consumers. We need to ask if there is a danger of personal data usage inadvertently doing the opposite of its original intention – potentially creating highly transactional relationships rather than ones which are richer and more rewarding.

Just as there are inevitably upsides for brands in the way they use personal data there are also challenges that need to be considered. This is a call for a more nuanced and thoughtful debate, not a rejection of the use of personal data.

Brands need to better understand where the boundaries lie in their use of personal data to avoid falling into an uncanny valley. These will vary by brand, category, customer segment, marketing channel and so on. More work needs to be done to understand what brands can do to mitigate the downside. Maybe greater access and control. Maybe a fundamentally different exchange of values based on insights gleaned through the data. A lot needs exploring and uncovering.

We also need to understand the degree to which brands are in danger of 'flattening' their relationships with consumers, perhaps unintentionally creating a less engaged and loyal customer base. Just because the effects may be subtle and therefore hard to identify does not mean we should not be exploring the possibilities of their existence, suggested by the literature and available research.

We are at the start of this particular journey, with more questions than answers, so we are not at a point where we can recommend best practice. This chapter is instead a manifesto for brands to become more engaged with the debate and start grappling with the nuanced issues around data-mediated relationships. As personal data becomes an ever-more important asset to make best use of, a comprehensive understanding of the way it shapes relationships looks set to be a key differentiator of success or failure.

Notes

1 Strong, Colin (2013) Big Marketing GfK and *The Guardian* [online] http://www.gfk.com/Documents/Big%20Marketing%20executive%20summary.pdf

2 Strong, Colin (2013) What is the future for online advertising? *Huffington Post* [online] http://www.huffingtonpost.co.uk/colin-strong/online-advertising_b_4269606.html

3 For more information on the availability heuristic see Kahneman, Daniel (2012) *Thinking Fast and Slow*, Penguin

4 Cyber spies in London recycle bins told to move on, *The Guardian*, 15 August 2013 [online] http://www.theguardian.com/media-network/partner-zone-infosecurity/cyber-spies-london-recycle-bins

5 Vallance, Chris (2014) NHS Care.data information scheme 'mishandled', *BBC* [online] http://www.bbc.com/news/health-27069553

6 Ariely, Dan (2009) *Predictably Irrational: The hidden forces that shape our decisions*, HarperCollins

7 For more information on the endowment effect see Kahneman, Daniel (2012) *Thinking Fast and Slow*, Penguin

8 Sengupta, Somini (2013) Letting our guard down over web privacy, *New York Times*, 31 March [online] http://www.nytimes.com/2013/03/31/technology/web-privacy-and-how-consumers-let-down-their-guard.html?pagewanted=all&_r=0

9 Mori, Masahiro (1970) The Uncanny Valley, *Energy* 7 (4), pp 33–35, available online at http://www.movingimages.info/digitalmedia/wp-content/uploads/2010/06/MorUnc.pdf

10 Fast Company (2011) Did the 'Uncanny Valley' kill Disney's CGI company? March 31 [online] http://www.fastcodesign.com/1663530/did-the-uncanny-valley-kill-disneys-cgi-company

11 Schrage, Michael (2013) When digital marketing gets to creepy, *HBR Blog Network*, June [online] http://blogs.hbr.org/2013/06/digital-marketings-big-custome/

12 Luft, J and Ingham, H (1955) The Johari window: a graphic model of interpersonal awareness, Proceedings of the Western training laboratory in group development, UCLA

13 Watson, Sara M (2014) Data doppelgängers and the uncanny valley of personalization, *The Atlantic*, 16 June [online] http://www.theatlantic.com/technology/archive/2014/06/data-doppelgangers-and-the-uncanny-valley-of-personalization/372780/

14 Chambers, Chris (2013) NSA and GCHQ: the flawed psychology of government mass surveillance, *The Guardian*, 26 August [online] http://www.theguardian.com/science/head-quarters/2013/aug/26/nsa-gchq-psychology-government-mass-surveillance

15 Smith, M J, Carayon, P, Sanders, K J, Lim, S-Y and LeGrande, D (1992) Employee stress and health complaints in jobs with and without electronic performance monitoring, *Applied Ergonomics* 23 (1), pp 17–27

16 Abrams, Dominic, Wetherell, Margaret, Cochrane, Sandra, Hogg, Michael A and Turner, John C (1990) Knowing what to think by knowing who you are: self-categorization and the nature of norm formation, conformity and group polarization, *British Journal of Social Psychology* 29 (2), pp 97–119

17 Buber, Martin (1937) *I and Thou*, Charles Scribner's Sons. Reprinted by Continuum International Publishing Group, 2004

18 Avery, Jill, Fournier, Susan and Wittenbraker, John (2014) Unlock the mysteries of your customer relationships, HBR *Blog Network*, July [online] http://hbr.org/2014/07/unlock-the-mysteries-of-your-customer-relationships/

19 Turkle, Sherry (2011) *Alone Together*, Basic Books

20 Appleyard, Bryan (2012) *The Brain is Wider Than the Sky: Why simple solutions don't work in a complex world*, Phoenix

21 Carr, Nicholas (2008) Is Google making us stupid? *The Atlantic Magazine*, 1 July [online] http://www.theatlantic.com/magazine/archive/2008/07/is-google-making-us-stupid/306868/

22 Duhigg, Charles (2012) How companies learn your secrets, *New York Times*, 16 Feb [online] http://www.nytimes.com/2012/02/19/magazine/shopping-habits.html?pagewanted=all

23 Ctrl-Shift (2014) The rise of the consumer empowering intermediary, *Consumer Futures* [online] http://www.consumerfutures.org.uk/files/2014/01/The-Rise-of-the-Consumer-Empowering-Intermediary-Ctrl-Shift.pdf

Getting personal

12

We talked in Chapter 1 about the way in which the increasing 'datafication' of our lives will fundamentally change the way in which brands and governments operate. This chapter looks at the challenges and opportunities that might exist when placing that data in the hands of the consumers themselves – the so-called shift from the big data economy to a personal data economy.

There has been an assumption that personal analytics, where individuals make use of their own personal data, will facilitate better decisions. Indeed, this assumption underpins UK government policy for midata, the scheme which entitles individuals to access the core contract, transaction and consumption history data that a service provider collects and holds about them.[1]

If personal analytics delivers on its promise, then it has potential to revolutionize the way in which brands and governments go about collecting, managing and analysing the data they hold on individuals. Expectations will significantly change and, to borrow a term from Doc Searls, one of the leading thinkers of the Personal Information Economy movement, the individual will increasingly be in control.[2] It follows that there will be a shift away from CRM (Customer Relationship Management) to VRM (Vendor Relationship Management), reflecting the changing balance of power in the relationship between individuals and organizations.

Despite the excitement of a rapidly changing data environment and the discussion about how this will play out, relatively little has been written about the individual end user. This chapter explores the degree to which individuals are able to take up the challenge and opportunities that the availability of personal data in their own hands might represent. Are individuals equipped to make the 'right' decisions in a world where they have so much data at their disposal? And if not, what should be done to support effective decision-making?

History of self-tracking

In the late 16th century the Italian physiologist and professor Santorio Santorio of the University of Padau, Italy, was engaged in an extraordinary experiment. For 30 years he not only weighed himself on a daily basis but also all the food and drink he consumed as well as the urine and faeces he subsequently produced. He then compared the weight of what he had consumed to that of his waste products and developed theories to account for the difference.

While the scientific theories that he developed to explain his measurements have long been debunked, it was one of the first recorded examples of 'self-tracking'. Since then there have been many other attempts by individuals to better understand themselves and their fellow human beings through recording their own behaviours. Allen Neuringer[3] provides an interesting account of the many examples that followed Santorio, including Anton Stork, who drank hemlock to understand its therapeutic effects, Henry Head, who cut the nerves in his arm to study the regeneration of pain and Herman Ebbinghaus, who conducted a series of memory experiments on himself over a two-year period. Some of these findings have fallen by the wayside, but others, such as Ebbinghaus' work, continue to be relevant.

The tracking of self-behaviours is not limited to scientists either. Athletes have long kept diaries of their food intake, training sessions, sleeping patterns and so on to improve their understanding of what factors may explain their performance. People with chronic health conditions have used similar means to help manage their symptoms.

However, as in many spheres, technology is promising to be a major source of disruption in the area of personal analytics. It's well documented how the cost of computing hardware has fallen dramatically to the point that analytics capabilities, once the preserve of large companies and governments that could afford mainframes in the basements of their buildings, are increasingly available at an individual level.[4]

Similarly, the internet has fundamentally changed the way in which information now flows in society. Pre-internet, the dominant information flows were mainly 'top-down' but now the internet facilitates both peer-to-peer, as well as bottom-up communication from individuals to organizations. Technology is also capturing ever more intimate aspects of our lives with mobile devices used to record sound and images, changes in direction and speed as well as taking biometric measurements.

In other words, all the ingredients are now available to record and analyse our lives in a way that our ancestors such as Santorio Santorio could not even have dreamed of. We are now seeing an explosion in the means that individuals now have available for tracking their own, often very intimate behaviours.

A changing personal data landscape

There is little doubt that the marriage of technology with self-insight has generated real momentum in the form of the Quantified Self (QS) movement. Launched in 2007 by *Wired* magazine editors Gary Wolf and Kevin Kelly, QS was billed as 'a collaboration of users and tool makers who share an interest in self-knowledge through self-tracking'.[5] Once considered the preserve of data geeks, the movement is now getting mainstream interest.[6] There is now a wide range of technology that individuals can purchase to capture their own behaviour both online and in traditionally off-line environments.

There have also been considerable developments in the regulatory environment that have contributed to the wider availability and distribution of personal data. For instance, a number of governments have been exploring how they can encourage institutions to make their data available to their citizens. In some cases this is in the form of access to governmental 'open data', which might be anything from bus times to rubbish collection.

But, more interestingly for the purposes of this chapter, it is also about releasing transaction data back to individuals. In the UK, as mentioned in Chapter 2, the government's midata programme is about engaging with brands (particularly in telecoms, banking, retail, and energy sectors) to provide individuals with their data in a 'machine-readable transportable format'.[7] Similar programmes are underway in other countries most notably in the United States and France.

The market for tracking health and fitness behaviours is growing rapidly with brands such as Fitbit, Jawbone and Nike competing in a growing global wearables market that is predicted to reach as much as US $19 billion by 2018.[8] These services allow the user to set goals and then provide feedback about performance against them. So, for example, the Fitbit app lets you know that just a few more steps will get you to your daily target with the aim of generally helping to 'nudge' you towards a healthy lifestyle.

These ecosystems are becoming increasingly sophisticated, allowing feeds from other sources such as wi-fi scales and apps that use GPS to plot routes, measure speed and distance and so on. These can often be used to link to a user's social network so they can compete with their friends if so desired.

The energy market is also being 'datafied', with smart meters being introduced into homes. Some US companies such as OPOWER have claimed success in the use of energy usage data, analytics and behavioural science, helping to reduce energy consumption in participating households.[9] In the UK, Smart Energy GB has been set up by the government and funded by energy companies in the expectation that it will 'finally let consumers get their energy consumption under control'.[10] Google's purchase of Nest, a 'smart' device to track and personalize energy usage in the household has had huge coverage, reflecting the level of interest in this area.

Given these market conditions there is a lot of excitement around personal analytics. The question is whether there is any evidence that having greater access to your own data means that individuals will actually be able to make better decisions. The next section considers this challenge.

The relationship between data ownership and empowerment

There are some questions that should be asked concerning actual usage of the data now available to individuals. There is some evidence that best intentions are not necessarily followed through with behaviour. In research undertaken by the author in 2014, of those that had used a tracking fitness device for less than six months an impressive 88 per cent claimed they used it at least once a week.

However, when questioning those that had had a device for six months or longer, the percentage using it at least once a week had fallen to 62 per cent. Similarly, after six months the numbers considering that their behaviours had changed 'a lot' or 'moderately' as a result of using the device had fallen from 78 per cent (those who had been using it for less than six months) to 61 per cent (those who had been using it for six months or longer). While these numbers cannot of course be considered evidence that fitness devices do not deliver any behavioural change, the results are somewhat lukewarm given that we need to bear in mind this is a group that are in the 'early mass adoption' wave and therefore motivated to maximize their usage of these devices.

Nor are the available results for engagement with energy efficiency compelling. OPOWER estimates that the percentage of customers that log on to explore their energy usage online is 'well below 5 per cent'. And although this results in a '2 per cent to 4 per cent aggregate energy savings' this doesn't provide a particularly powerful business case for the personal analytics economy.[11]

It's hard to say at this stage whether there is any variability in the propensity of consumers to engage with data sources to drive decision-making as a function of demographic or market category. Of course, for example, in some categories it may be easier to take the necessary steps than others (turning down a thermostat is easier than taking more exercise) and some demographic groups my feel more confident about taking the necessary steps. These issues certainly merit further exploration.

Nevertheless, the current evidence, as it stands, does point to a reluctance by consumers to engage with data, failing to translate analysis into changed behaviour or indeed to maintain their interest in the collection and analysis of data. We now explore some of the possible reasons for this.

The pitfalls of personal analytics

This section explores three possible barriers to effective engagement and usage of personal data and analytics; the psychology of inertia, our cognitive ability to make sense of the data and the pitfalls of 'data overload'.

The psychology of inertia

It can seem as though humans are wired for inertia, with our cognitive 'rules of thumb', the means by which we effectively navigate the world, focusing us on short-term, loss-averse behaviours. This does not always work in our favour, particularly when the benefits operate over the longer term and are less salient than the shorter-term task. Examples of this include:[12]

- 'Hyperbolic discounting'. This is the tendency to over-emphasize short-term costs over long-term benefits. So the work involved in constantly tracking behaviour and then taking remedial action is a salient short-term cost in comparison with a longer-term goal of, for example, optimizing spend or being fitter.

- 'Regret aversion'. This is where individuals are worried about making a decision that they fear they will come to regret in the future. The concern is not only with what they have but how it compares to what they *might have had*. So taking the time for personal analytics and subsequent action may mean other things are neglected that it is feared may come to be regretted.

- 'Social effects'. The actions of others can have a significant effect on individuals' decision-making process. So awareness of others that do not engage in personal analytics or perhaps do not follow through with behaviour change can have a significant influence on individuals' propensity to do so themselves.

- 'Choice overload'. There is much evidence that when presented with a large number of options or information then the resulting confusion from extra information is distracting and may lead individuals to passivity or poor decisions.

So despite all the opportunities that increasing access to personal data seems to offer, there are many ways in which cognitive processes seem to mitigate the opportunities presented by this data, resulting in inertia.

Making sense of data

There is little value in having personal data available to us if we are not able to interpret it correctly. Of course there are services that help us to do just that but nevertheless some degree of interpretation of the data is still typically needed. As we saw in Chapter 5, we are not always well equipped to draw conclusions about the data we are presented with. As such, analysis of personal data can result in spurious activity and therefore ineffective outcomes.

Information overload

We have a natural assumption that the more information we have available to us, the better the decision. The proliferation of personal data now available certainly appears to reflect this theme – surely if individuals have more data then, notwithstanding the previous points, there is at least greater potential to reach the best possible outcomes.

This is, however, a view that psychologist Gerd Gigerenzer[13] would disagree with, in fact suggesting that ignorance can sometimes benefit people attempting to make inferences from their knowledge. A good example of this is a study by Goldstein and Gigerenzer[14] who asked both American and German students which was the bigger city: San Antonio or San Diego? Just 62 per cent of the Americans correctly named San Diego – but the German students were uniformly correct.

All of the German students had heard of San Diego but only about half had heard of San Antonio. Half of the German students would therefore be able to apply a recognition heuristic – if you recognize one and not the other, then it makes sense to pick the city you recognize. As people usually hear about the bigger cities of foreign countries before the smaller ones – ie, recognition correlates with the criterion being predicted – this cue does actually work. Because the American students had heard of both cities they couldn't use this cue and had to rely on other, apparently less effective, cues. In terms of accuracy, it seems, when it comes to using knowledge to make inferences, less can sometimes mean more.

Gigerenzer suggests that much of the time we can overcomplicate the way in which we make decisions, trying to take a wide range of different variables into account and weight them appropriately. But in reality taking a small number of factors will result in a quality of decision that is, for the most part, good enough – 'satisficing' instead of 'maximizing'. Indeed, maximizing can have unexpected negative effects. A hospital in Michigan was the setting for a study[15] exploring just this issue. In this case doctors concerned with possible liabilities associated with claims of under-treatment were sending large numbers of patients with chest pains straight to the coronary care unit. The problem was that this not only cost the hospital more but of course the patients ran higher risks of infection. The hospital had carefully introduced a complex decision support system to allocate patients more efficiently, but the doctors disliked it and so went back to defensive decision-making.

Gigerenzer developed a much simpler decision tree that asked the doctors just three yes/no questions about each patient's electrocardiographs and other data. Compared with both the complex decision support system and the status quo, this 'fast and frugal' method of decision-making helped the doctors to send more patients to the coronary care unit who belonged there and fewer who did not. Doctors were able to use a small number of 'smart heuristics' or rules of thumb that determined the appropriate activity in a simple yet effective manner.

It can be argued, therefore, that more information does not necessarily empower, instead it reduces effectiveness and, as mentioned earlier, can result in inertia. This is increasingly understood by organizations. Terms such as 'infobesity' describe the way that despite the huge amount of data now available to us we often struggle to manage and make sense of it all. Exactly the same principles apply to individuals trying to make sense of their own personal data.

Potential solutions for empowerment

It is increasingly apparent that empowering individuals is not simply a matter of granting access to their personal data. There are not insignificant barriers to effective usage which can result in inertia, confusion or the wrong decisions being made. To this end we now explore two possible ways in which organizations may wish to enhance individuals' decision-making in the area of personal data – one which engages with the psychology of decision-making and another which involves the use of technology to facilitate decision support and, indeed, subsequent activity.

The psychology of decision-making

As mentioned earlier, we often look to our experience to help us make short cuts to navigate the world, based on years of trial and error. This means that we can quickly and easily assimilate a wide range of different pieces of information using heuristics, simple rules of thumb, to determine how best to act. Much of the time this is done unconsciously and is given the label 'intuition'. Gigerenzer cites the example[16] of baseball players that rely on the gaze heuristic which is to 'Fix your gaze on an object, and adjust your speed so that the angle of gaze remains constant'. This simple rule allows the baseball player to react swiftly and intuitively:

> The player does not need to calculate the trajectory of the ball. To select the right parabola, the player's brain would have to estimate the ball's initial distance, velocity and angle, which is not a simple feat. And to make things more complicated, real-life balls do not fly in parabolas. Wind, air resistance, and spin affect their paths. Even the

most sophisticated robots or computers today cannot correctly estimate a landing point during the few seconds a ball soars through the air.
The gaze heuristic solves this problem by guiding the player toward the landing point, not by calculating it mathematically.

So at times 'smart heuristics', as Gigerenzer calls them, can lead to pretty good decisions. These appear to work well in situations where the information in the environment is diagnostic of the appropriate action. So, for example, if an individual runs more then she knows she gets fitter. There is a feedback loop, developed over years, which gives the information of what is needed that works quickly and effectively. However, if an individual wants to get really fit, for example if she is running competitively and trying to shave a few seconds off her marathon times, then the feedback loops are complex and not experienced previously. She cannot rely on the rules of thumb in order to understand what to do. So in novel or complicated environments smart heuristics do not operate so effectively. But in many situations they are often good enough.

This is important in the context of consumer analytics as it could be argued that technology over-engineers the consumer decision. Does a consumer really need a data read-out on their thermostat to reduce their home heating bill when most people can quickly and with little information from their environment know how to manage the heating in their homes so they can maximize the relationship between their comfort and minimum energy usage? We are typically in environments where we can quickly make sensible decisions with minimal information – we are able to operate in a fast and frugal manner.

This type of 'fast and frugal' decision-making is much more widespread than might be realized. An interesting study by Mandeep Dhami and Peter Ayton looked at 'bail or jail' decisions made by UK magistrates, who are required to take a large number of factors into account when deciding whether to remand offenders in jail or to release them on bail.[17] The study found that magistrates typically took just two or three factors into consideration despite their protestations to the contrary.

Another study by the author explored whether fast and frugal decision-making is operating in purchase choices. These sorts of decisions are different from those typically explored by decision scientists since the issue is not whether something is factually right or wrong but requires the individual to arrive at a purchase decision based on personal preference. The study compared how well a fast and frugal model and a compensatory model, one which involved weighting of a wide number of factors, could predict choices between television sets.

The findings showed that a fast and frugal model of the decision-making process (based on just one single product feature) can make relatively good predictions of choice, compared to much more complex models. This suggests that for much of the time fast and frugal decision-making is used to parse the information to reach a purchase.

Knowing this has important implications for consumer decision-making. Organizations that champion consumer rights may, for example, want to help side-step the complex detail that is often presented when changing energy supplier, with guidance that provides a handful of simple questions that facilitate a 'good enough' decision. At the moment the 'feedback loops' for consumers may not be quick enough to gather cues from the environment to enable fast and frugal decision-making. But our propensity to try to make such decisions can be recognized and worked. Whilst it may not necessarily maximize the decision process, it can provide an outcome that is probably better than the current status quo, which is to do nothing.

Technology-based decision support

An alternative approach to helping to facilitate personal decision-making is via a new breed of technology companies. These are intermediaries that sit between brands and individuals to help find the best deal – so they deal with the 'personal analytics' on the user's behalf. While the first generation of intermediaries, price comparison sites, are well known, they are typically limited in their current form. They focus almost solely on price and are limited to reviewing one service at a time.

A new type of intermediary, the 'next generation', has a more rounded offer in terms of the analytics they employ. They not only look at price and supplier performance from third-party rating sites but also use personal data that has been volunteered by individuals about their preferences. Along with employing a wider range of information, the fundamental business model is changing from a one-off or occasional use to an ongoing relationship that checks the individual has the right tariff with the right supplier, and not just for one, but for a whole range of services.

These services often claim to offer continual assurance that the user is getting the best deal on the terms specified in advance (whether that be level of price saving, ethical reputation of suppliers, quality of service etc). Importantly, they are increasingly expected to do the actual switching on individuals' behalf when a better supplier is found.

Examples of these sorts of intermediaries include:

- Incahoot's concierge service, which analyses household bills as a basis for then overhauling household finances;

- Intently, which allows individuals to broadcast their purchase intentions to the market, letting sellers approach them in a privacy-friendly way;

- Cheap Energy Club, which monitors the changing tariffs in the energy market and alerts their users when they identify an opportunity to generate cost savings to the level that has been specified.

The sheer scale and complexity of the choice now facing individuals for even the most simple of purchases means people are ever more willing to delegate decision-making to these intermediaries or 'choice engines',[18] as Richard Thaler and Will Tucker have called them in an influential article on the topic. For example, the Cheap Energy Club, part of the UK website MoneySavingExpert.com, while not offering some of the more advanced attributes of other next generation intermediaries (such as actually switching to the new tariff), constantly monitors the market and makes sure their (over one million) users have the best deals.

On this basis inertia, the driver of stickiness, then actually works in favour of the individual as a recent Consumer Futures report[19] points out:

> If the key to more efficient, effective markets is not so much to 'change' consumer behaviour but to accept the reality of behaviours as they are

and compensate for them, the maturing intermediary services market may be a catalyst for more widespread market changes.

Concluding thoughts

As the amount of data available on our lives massively grows, it is tempting to think that with this comes a rise in our ability to make effective decisions, that we are increasingly 'empowered'. It is more and more clear, however, that having information available is often a necessary, but not sufficient, condition of being able to make a good decision.

So how should organizations help individuals make good choices based on their data? The findings of this study present two possible solutions. The first, using fast and frugal methods to help navigate the morass of information, is one that is surely compelling as it is potentially low in cost and has a track record of effective outcomes. Here the requirement is to understand the key information that is needed to make a decision that is 'good enough' so individuals can employ rules of thumb that work in their favour. In situations where there is an absolute, rational outcome this is easy to model and implement. In the hospital example of allocating medical treatments, it is possible to establish the accuracy of the prediction and the degree of false positives. This is an important and useful finding for regulators hoping to encourage more switching activity in their markets.

In the cases where personal preference comes into play it is somewhat harder. However, in the example of using fast and frugal decision trees to guide individuals to their preferred television set, initial evidence certainly found some evidence that they can be effective in modelling choice for consumers. This is key information for brands that have historically used quite complex models involving a wide range of attributes including product features, pricing, service levels and so on. The reality that decision-making is likely much simpler provides an opportunity to focus marketing efforts in a much more effective manner.

Similarly, the learnings of 'fast and frugal' need to be taken on board by the sorts of services that hope to engender behaviour change. For example, fitness device brands may wish to explore how they can provide the few most effective pieces of data that will encourage positive behaviours and thereby reduce the high levels of drop-off in usage. Regulators can consider which pieces of information can be used to encourage individuals to look around the market and switch brands, thus tackling the low levels of churn in many regulated markets.

Next generation intermediaries offer an interesting alternative, as they essentially delegate the decision and subsequent activity to a third party. The success of price comparison sites certainly indicates the opportunity for these sorts of services to provide an elegant solution for those that don't feel equipped to engage with markets in an effective way. There are a host of regulatory issues associated with the effective implementation of these systems; for example, providing access to online transaction data may put individuals in breach of the terms and conditions of their service provider. But more pertinent to this paper, these services also have their own challenges concerning inertia. Will individuals be prepared to make the effort to sign up to them in the first place? The success of Cheap Energy Club suggests there are opportunities but there is more to be done to establish best practice in this area. Again, the underlying psychology of choice needs to be understood in the context of decision support services.

It is apparent that empowerment involves more than providing data – individuals need to have the tools to engage and make sense of that data. Real empowerment only comes when we better understand how to implement the psychology of decision-making in the real world.

Notes

1 Making midata a reality (2012) available at https://www.gov.uk/government/news/next-steps-making-midata-a-reality

2 Searls, Doc (2012) *The Intention Economy: When customers take charge*, Harvard Business Review Press

3 Neuringer, Allen (1981) Self-experimentation: a call for change, *Behaviourism*, **9** (1)

4 A history of storage cost (update) (2014) *Mkomo* [online] http://www.mkomo.com/cost-per-gigabyte-update

5 Read about the Quantified Self movement online at http://quantifiedself.com/about/

6 Fit, fit, hooray! (2014) *The Economist* [online] http://www.economist.com/blogs/babbage/2013/05/quantified-self

7 Making midata a reality (2012) (see note 1 above)

8 Reisinger, Don (2013) Wearable tech revenue to hit $19B by 2018, *cnet* [online] http://www.cnet.com/uk/news/wearable-tech-revenue-to-hit-19b-by-2018/2014

9 Laskey, Alex and Kavaazovic, Ogi (2010) Energy efficiency through behavioural science and technology, *opower* [online] https://opower.com/uploads/library/file/15/xrds_opower.pdf XRDS

10 Joseph, Seb (2014) Energy industry unveils £85m plan to tout smart meter benefits, *Marketing Week* [online] http://www.marketingweek.co.uk/sectors/utilities/news/energy-industry-unveils-85m-plan-to-tout-smart-meter-benefits/4011020.article

11 Laskey, Alex and Kavaazovic, Ogi (2010) (see note 9 above)

12 Khaneman, Daniel (2011) *Thinking Fast and Slow*, Penguin

13 Gigerenzer, Gerd (2014) *Risk Savvy: How to make good decisions*, Allen Lane

14 Goldstein, Daniel G and Gigerenzer, Gerd (2002) Models of ecological rationality: the recognition heuristic, *Psychological Review* 109, pp 75–90

15 Gigerenzer, Gerd and Kerzenhäauser, Stephanie (2005) Fast and frugal heuristics in medical decision making, in Bibace, R, Laird, J D, Noller, K L and Valsiner, J (eds), *Science and Medicine in Dialogue* (pp 3–15), Praeger

16 Gigerenzer, Gerd (2014) (see note 13 above)

17 Dhami, Mandeep and Ayton, Peter (2001) Bailing and jailing the fast and frugal way, *Journal of Behavioural Decision Making* 14 (2), pp 141–68

18 Thaler, Richard T and Tucker, Will (2013) Smarter information, smarter consumers, *Harvard Business Review* (Jan–Feb)

19 Ctrl-shift (2014) The rise of the consumer empowering intermediary, *Consumer Futures* [online] http://www.consumerfutures.org.uk/files/2014/01/The-Rise-of-the-Consumer-Empowering-Intermediary-Ctrl-Shift.pdf

Privacy paradox

13

There is no shortage of discussion about privacy, not least because we are all starting to realize just how complicated a topic it is. Nor is there an easy answer as to how to go about managing it. What is clear, however, is that brands need to engage properly with the topic and find that delicate balance between gathering and using data when attempting to forge closer customer relationships without overstepping the mark, thus leading to consumer alienation. This is by no means straightforward, since many consumers declare they are concerned with privacy while simultaneously giving away vast amounts of personal information with what at times appears to be reckless abandon.

We have to begin somewhere, however. A good place to start may be with teenagers, because the almost universally-held view is that, despite their protestations, they simply don't care enough about online privacy. Yet though there seems to be evidence of this,[1] teenagers also use social media in ways at odds with their apparent attitudes. This is the so-called 'privacy paradox', and it can have disastrous consequences.[2] In the UK, for example, Paris Brown famously felt obliged to resign as the country's first Police Youth Crime Commissioner after some ill-advised tweets she had made some years previously. Other cases have tragically involved teens taking their lives after being blackmailed over personal footage posted online. Whilst these are the more extreme examples, many who have contact with teenagers are aware of instances where they have not appeared to have sufficient concern for their privacy.

This is an important demographic to explore in this context because it has huge implications for brands. If teens are playing fast and loose with their privacy then, it is argued, surely this indicates more general societal changes? Indeed, Facebook's Mark Zuckerberg has claimed that privacy is no longer a social norm, using this to justify changing the network's privacy settings.[3] If, however, the assumption that teenagers are unconcerned about online privacy is wrong, then this has much wider implications for the way in which brands use personal data.

This chapter explores that complex relationship between consumers, brands and privacy.

Teenagers and privacy

The reality is that, far from being careless about their privacy, teenagers manage it carefully. They just aren't so obvious about it. Research studies among teenagers reveal that the vast majority agree that there are some things they just would not post, and that they would also be wary of putting anything inappropriate online. Of course, self-censorship doesn't always work out and over half of those researched say they sometimes delete things they have posted.

As with previous generations, teens will always make mistakes when experimenting socially. There are just much greater privacy consequences today. The teens surveyed certainly felt the tension between being able to express themselves spontaneously and freely while simultaneously having to worry about being private (a facet reflected in the findings from Pew Research[4] in the United States).

Teens also use quite sophisticated means to manage privacy, relying on social coding rather than the more formal means available through, for example, a site's privacy settings. This is often in the form of in-jokes, which people will ignore or misunderstand unless they are part of the intended recipient group, or dirtying data by putting in false personal details.

Another form of coding is 'vaguebooking', or using an intentionally vague Facebook status such as 'Why would you do this to me?' This is meant to prompt friends to ask what is happening, rather than having to post detailed information upfront. As Danah Boyd, a principal researcher at Microsoft Research, puts it:[5] 'The point is to allow access to the content but zero access to the meaning' so that its significance is understood by only a select group of peers.

Another key means that teens use to manage their privacy is to separate their online connections by using different networks. When teens feel they have too many of a particular circle of friends or have family members on some social networks, they divert to other networks to gain some privacy and to feel more able to express themselves more freely. So it is an increasingly common route for teenagers, as they get older, to start to find their Facebook presence is over-populated by family and too wide a circle of friends, so they start to migrate to sites which more naturally exclude others, such as Twitter or Snapchat.

Boyd has written extensively[6] about how teenagers use 'social stenography' to help manage their privacy online. This is worth reading for those wanting to gain a deeper understanding of the nuances of the issues involved with this demographic group.

The pros and cons of data disclosure

So it seems teenagers do care about privacy as much as everyone else and find ways to avoid too much disclosure. However, before we consider the problems that privacy and consumer attitudes towards it present, let's look briefly at how consumers can both win and lose from sharing personal data. On the positive side, consumers can enjoy:[7]

- free content or services: Google and Facebook's services are predicted on this business model;
- personalized services: the obvious example here is Amazon's recommendation service but also, more generally, increasingly relevant and timely marketing;
- reduced search costs: Google has revolutionized our ability to access information;
- more efficient interactions with merchants or their sites: so, for example, we don't have to keep repeating the same basic information about ourselves.

Other benefits may accrue which are not specific to the individual consumer such as:

- enhanced consumer data may allow brands to reduce the amount of marketing investment wasted on consumers uninterested in the product, potentially leading to lower product prices;

- aggregation of web searches of many individuals could help detect disease outbreaks;

- aggregation of location data could be used to improve traffic conditions and reduce road congestion.

But there are costs consumers can face from both privacy violations and disclosed data. Ryan Calo of the University of Washington[8] distinguishes between subjective and objective privacy harms. He cites the work of a leading authority in the psychology of privacy, economist Alessandro Acquisti,[9] who talks of subjective harm as relating to 'the anticipation of losing control of personal data: so can include anxiety, embarrassment or fear; the psychological discomfort associated with feeling surveilled; the embarrassment associated with public exposure of sensitive information; or the chilling effects of fearing one's personal life will be intruded upon.'

The objective harms, meanwhile, 'can be immediate and tangible, or indirect and intangible' and range from damage caused by identity theft to time spent dealing with annoying telemarketing.

According to Acquisti, there are three main ways[10] in which consumers can suffer from data disclosure:

- Consumers can make mistakes as they don't fully understand what might happen if they reveal too much about themselves, lacking the spread of knowledge about data collection and its uses that major corporates possess.

- The life cycle in which personal data operates is now so complex it is impossible for individuals to work out when best to disclose such data and when to keep it to ourselves.

- Even if we were able to access complete information and the cognitive power to process it exhaustively, cognitive biases will typically lead to behaviours that are systematically different from those predicted by rational choice theory.

So consumers are often not in a position to gauge the consequences of disclosing personal information. But further, it seems we don't necessarily have stable preferences for privacy given it covers so many different contexts. Is someone getting a glimpse of your naked body on a par with someone knowing what you purchased in the supermarket yesterday? There are so many different elements to calculating the costs of privacy violation that it's fair to say that our preferences are uncertain. And when our preferences are uncertain, decision-making is much more likely to be influenced by factors that are not strictly 'rational' such as the way in which the different options are described, or 'framed'. As such, to better understand our behaviours around privacy and disclosure we need to better understand the behavioural economics of privacy.

The behavioural economics of privacy

This is an area we touched on in Chapter 11, where we looked at the challenges facing brands. One important finding discussed was that when leveraging value from personal data they have collected, brands can find that social and market norms collide. This can at times have a damaging impact on brands involved because of the different expectations that are generated.

We also touched on the endowment effect, which occurs when individuals place a much greater value on the goods that they own than on the identical products that they don't own. Acquisti's research found just such an effect in relation to privacy and personal data. Different offers were put to shoppers in Pittsburgh in the United States.[11] Some were given a choice of a $10 discount card, plus $2 more discount if they revealed their shopping details. Some 50 per cent said no to the $2 extra offer, considering it insufficient incentive. Other shoppers got a slightly different offer: a $12 discount card, which they could trade in for $10 if they wanted to keep their shopping data private. This time round 90 per cent opted to keep the $12 card, even if it meant revealing personal data.

This is classic endowment effect: people attach a much greater weight to the price asked if an organization wishes to buy their data than they would be willing to spend to ensure it was not released. This sense of ownership erects barriers to parting with their data too easily.

Another study explored the so-called illusion of control. Here, people are likely to disclose much more personal information if they sense that controls are in place. One might of course expect this but

what is less logical is that the presence of controls has a disproportionate impact on the willingness of individuals to disclose data.

Acquisti and colleagues asked in a study[12] whether participants
had ever stolen, lied or taken drugs. Then the group was split into
three, with each given a different scenario. The first were told that
their answers would appear in a research bulletin; the second would
be able to give explicit permission about whether to publish those
answers, while the third group would be asked for their permission
but would also have to give their age, sex and country of birth.

The first group were, not surprisingly, the most reluctant to reveal
personal data, while those whose permission was sought were nearly
twice as likely to answer all the questions. As for those prompted
to give demographic data, every single person volunteered it, even
though those details could have allowed a complete stranger a greater
chance of identifying the participant. So we seem to overstate the
importance of controls in our mind, perversely putting more into the
public domain than we would otherwise have done.

So the way in which we make decisions concerning privacy is not
fixed or independent of the context in which we find ourselves. This
makes privacy a complex issue for consumers and brands alike. It
raises important questions such as: what is the appropriate use of
data? How can a brand be sure it is not overstepping the mark? What
happens to brands that do overstep the mark? To what extent is trust
in the brand damaged? It's becoming apparent that the answers to
this are subtle and highly dependent on context.

The behavioural economics of privacy for teenagers

In an ideal world we trade off short- and long-term costs and
benefits in a balanced manner. In reality, we all place much greater
importance on the short rather than the long term. But young people,
not unsurprisingly, are more susceptible to this, as are those in an
emotional state or who are distracted. So the short-term excitement of
posting something inappropriate is far more important than the long-
term consequences. While we are all vulnerable to this, teenagers are
more so than others.

Teenagers are also more vulnerable to the 'illusion of privacy'. Somewhat perversely, research has found that the finer the privacy controls – and hence the greater the sense of control on any online site – then the more likely people are to share sensitive information with larger audiences. Most teenagers are over-optimistic about the degree to which they have understood and made appropriate use of online privacy settings, so de facto they are in greater danger of placing inappropriate information in front of a wide audience (in spite of their clear preference for privacy as noted earlier).

But perhaps most important is the notion of 'coherent arbitrariness'. In most spheres of decision-making we tend to look to our environment for cues on what the appropriate response should be. Here, quite subtle and unconscious cues can arbitrarily influence our behaviour: famously, asking people for the last two digits of their credit card can impact valuations of a bottle of wine as we are then unconsciously adopting an (albeit random) anchor for our subsequent valuations. We quickly adapt, however, using our price estimate to drive coherence, framing future decisions about other bottles of wine relative to the value of our initial estimate.

And this is exactly the way in which attitudes to privacy work. Most people don't really know what their preferences are relating to privacy but will frame the appropriateness of their behaviour quickly based on changes in the way their peers are managing their online privacy. So while only a minority of teenagers may fail to safeguard it, this can quickly become the new norm within the teen population.

Brand challenges

If consumers find it difficult to navigate privacy and make consistent decisions on what they consider to be right for them, brands may equally find it hard to predict how consumers will react to the ways in which their data is used. Indeed, brands are highly vulnerable on this topic, particularly given the received wisdom that the real value of data relates to its potential – and not just its current – usage.

As Cukier and Mayer-Schönberger argue:[13]

Data's true value is like an iceberg floating in the ocean. Only a tiny part of it is visible at first sight, while much of it is hidden beneath the surface. Innovative companies that understand this can extract that hidden value and reap potentially huge benefits. In short, data's value needs to be considered in terms of all the possible ways it can be employed in the future, not simply how it is used in the present.

Cukier and Mayer-Schönberger may set out a very cogent case for this, but part of the story is surely missing: how the consumer feels about this. As we saw earlier, part of consumers' concerns are typically about the way in which their data may be used in the future. As discussed in Chapter 11, brands might seek to have a close 'I–Thou' relationship. However, if customers sense uncertainty about how any personal data gathered might be used at some point in the future, it can harm the relationship.

Indeed, there is the potential for the marketing infrastructure that brands have built based on trust to crumble. Susan Fournier has long espoused the importance of relationships with her groundbreaking paper, 'Consumers and their brands',[14] published in 1998. Her research has established a clear framework for the evaluation of consumer–brand connections and examined the damage that a breakdown in trust can cause.

Together with colleagues Jennifer Aaker and S. Adam Brasel, she explored[15] what happens when things go wrong through a two-month field experiment in which 48 consumers formed a relationship with an online photographic service brand called Captura Photography Services. Two contrasting 'personalities' were created: one was 'sincere', with classic and traditional core values, the other 'exciting', with a more modern, irreverent feel.

Some 48 'customers' interacted with the service one to three times each week over the two-month period. But then they were told that a staff member had accidentally erased their online photos. Two days later they were sent apologies when the online albums were restored. What is particularly interesting is that the 'sincere' brand, which had developed strong bonds with its customers, suffered more in terms of customer perception than the 'exciting' service. After the apology and recovery, the latter was able to forge a better relationship with customers, allowing it to establish trust, accountability and responsibility in their minds for the first time.

As Aaker warns, when trust, which is central to successful marketing, is violated the effect on the brand can be devastating. This makes the issue of personal data and privacy critical to brand management since brands increasingly use personal data to build long-standing relationships with customers. To quote Aaker:

> When trust is violated – as it often is in long-standing relationships, particularly those established with a sincere, warm and honest partner – it can be devastating. So be aware of the type of brand partner you are, the type of relationship you are helping to create, and the expectations that are being set in the consumer's mind.

Nevertheless, brands that use personal data quite intensively will inevitably find themselves getting it wrong at some point. The impact this will have on a brand will clearly vary. But the message from Fournier's work is clear. Sincere brands that are attempting to generate trust will suffer the worst when they transgress because of raised expectations.

Trust frameworks and transparency

The approach to the drawing-up of terms and conditions that govern the use of personal data and, therefore, the way in which privacy is currently managed has been compared to a national rail network governed by standards that change every two feet by Alan Mitchell, from personal data consultancy Ctrl-Shift. Brands, he has argued, typically have their own independently drawn-up terms and conditions governing their use of personal data which are unique to their business but with no sense of consistency or interconnectedness with those from other brands.

Despite their complexity, consumers are expected to sign up to them before they can make their purchase or use services. Yet very few people actually read them. In fact, a poll undertaken among a representative sample of UK consumers found that 40 per cent of consumers agree that they never read any of those they signed up to online. This is despite 85 per cent of those same consumers considering it important to understand what information is held about them in those terms and conditions.[16]

The penalty of ignoring the small print

It might not seem the most exciting of subjects, but ignoring the terms and conditions can make a significant difference. Kyle Goodwin found this out to his cost. He used the now-defunct file-sharing site Megaupload as back-up storage for his Ohio-based film business, OhioSportsNet. This was a small business that filmed local sports events in schools and suchlike. When Megaupload was shut down in 2012 for alleged violation of copyright laws Goodwin, along with many others, was unable to access the material stored on the site.

Despite his best efforts the terms and conditions that he signed up to meant that he no longer had rights of ownership to materials stored there, so no possibility of a comeback. That's a pretty big handicap when trying to retrieve them.

This is the conundrum: polls show that consumers want a greater understanding of what they are signing up to. But they don't want to have to become legal experts. One solution might be the emerging concept of 'trust frameworks'. These are sets of commonly agreed rules, tools and infrastructure that enable parties in an ecosystem to do business with each other simply and securely. A standard set of rules and processes will exist for the sharing of information which all parties in the network understand and agree to work to.

The argument is that, if the consumer no longer has to shoulder tasks associated with privacy monitoring, checking, policing and risk-taking, they will be more confident when undertaking tasks online that they might not otherwise have engaged in. Similarly, the same benefits accrue to organizations, who can be confident that they can work with each other on the same 'trust framework' basis.

Of course, this will still present challenges. Any organization can set itself up as a provider of a 'trust framework'. Companies wishing to accelerate growth in new markets will see it as an attractive option, because it quickly establishes a way in which consumers can place faith in brands. However, there is also a credibility issue for a self-appointed 'trust framework' brand appointing themselves as rule makers. Do they, for example, have the resources and effective business model to gain market credibility and sustain this position? Such questions are, however, those that should be asked of any regulatory body.

Ctrl-Shift identifies three opportunities for brands[17] to benefit from 'trust frameworks'. Specifically:

- Enhanced efficiency: existing organizational processes can be run more efficiently because of the identity assurance that such frameworks provide.

- Rebuilding trust: organizations are encouraged to demonstrate their commitment to responsible data use.

- Springboard for innovation: as consumer trust grows, so they might consider sharing other rich data that could complement what brands already hold on them – in exchange for more relevant/enhanced services.

Clearly, benefits exist for consumers who don't need to understand the specifics of each brand's terms and conditions concerning the way in which their data will be used since they will be governed by a set of principles that the company has already agreed to abide by in relation to their personal data.

The trend towards transparency

Trust frameworks are, in effect, about providing greater transparency to consumers concerning the way their personal data is managed. Their development has much to do with the broad consensus for 'transparency and control' solutions arrived at by policy makers, industry and privacy advocates. It is manifest in the United States, in both the Federal Trade Commission white paper on consumer privacy[18] and with the White House Consumer Bill of Rights.[19] These promote transparency and notice as essential to consumer privacy protection.

Digital brands, such as Facebook and Google, have generally backed the approaches by policy-makers (although they have also attracted criticism for breaches of privacy). Indeed, Facebook has stated that '... companies should provide a combination of greater transparency and meaningful choice...' for consumers, with Google arguing that making the 'collection of personal information transparent' and giving users 'meaningful choices to protect their privacy' are two of its guiding privacy principles. Some privacy advocates have also embraced these approaches.[20]

But does transparency work?

An important paper by psychologists Idris Adjerid, Alessandro Acquisti, Laura Brandimarte and George Loewenstein[21] questioned the value of transparency and the idea that we can effectively place control in the hands of the user. In a series of experiments, they found that the impact of even simple and easily read privacy notices could easily be manipulated so they had the unintended effect of the consumer providing more personal information, rather than less.

The first experiment they conducted looked at the effects of framing the change in privacy protection as increasing or decreasing, even when the absolute risks of disclosure stay the same. Indeed, they found that, if online brands strongly emphasized increases in privacy protection, then consumers would offer more information than those in a control condition. Of course, this is common practice in the industry where brands tend to give consumers assurances of constantly improving privacy protection. In addition the study's authors also found that the effect of privacy notices on disclosure reduced over time. So whilst there may be an initial impact users quickly settle back into old disclosure habits after a short period.

In their second study, they found that the likelihood of privacy notices to influence disclosure can be reduced by simple 'misdirections'. An example of this is that a delay of just 15 seconds between the notice being given and the disclosure decision being required can have a significant impact on likelihood to accept the privacy terms being offered, and as such disclose more personal information. The study's authors argue that the kinds of manipulation captured by their experiment mimic the types of obstacle that consumers face when making privacy decisions online in the 'real world'. Examples of this are cited as a time gap between the reading of a notice and later requirement to make a decision whilst another common misdirection is when consumers are provided with a detailed notice and the ability to control some dimensions of their privacy preferences (such as the ability for other users to access their personal information), but a less detailed and salient notice and ability to control (if any) the collection and usage of their personal data by the service providers themselves.

So what should brands do?

The implications of the above research are clear – privacy notices can easily be manipulated so they have little or no effective influence on consumers' disclosure and privacy behaviours. Brands can clearly (and often do) use this to their advantage, often persuading consumers to exhibit ever greater levels of disclosure.

This is not to argue that greater transparency provided by initiatives such as Trust Frameworks are not important. Perhaps we can describe these as necessary but not sufficient conditions by which consumers can exercise their judgement.

To this end there is surely a case for communicating the risks for consumers to their privacy more clearly when they need them most, at the point at which they are called upon to disclose.

There is a large body of work by behavioural economists that identifies ways consumers can be helped to make more informed decisions with regard to their privacy. Thaler and Sunstein have trailblazed in this area, suggesting that policy-makers might use 'nudges to counteract known limitations in decision-making that may inhibit consumers' ability to make optimal decisions.[22] A 'nudge' uses or counters a known bias to help those consumers that exhibit limitations in their decision-making towards more informed and conscious decision. Adjerid *et al* suggest there may be opportunities for brands to provide default settings around privacy that are mindful of the current understanding of the way in which consumers make these decisions, and then counter consumers' limited attention spans by providing relevant notices at points of disclosure. So there may be value in intelligently informing consumers at points where they may be about to disclose information they may regret (very sensitive personal information or negative comments about other people). Also, before accepting invasive privacy terms and conditions for particular services, the choice could be briefly delayed to allow time to consider the trade-offs associated with the decision.

Concluding thoughts

It is increasingly clear that there is something deeply flawed about the concept of transparency as being a panacea to the challenges of privacy. The weight of the psychology literature clearly demonstrates that we are not well equipped to always make the right decision when faced with a complex set of information and contexts to navigate. And how can we even know what the right decision is when we do not know the future uses to which data will be put?

And getting it right is not just an issue for consumers. It is increasingly clear that brands face real downsides for making the wrong call. Given the complexity of the privacy issues to be navigated, then occasionally they inevitably will. And all the work that has gone into building trust in the brand will, almost unfairly it seems, then work against the brand in the ensuing backlash.

Possibly the question is whether brands are brave enough to open up a dialogue with consumers as to how their relationship should evolve. Would brands really do this? It is currently difficult to imagine when the business models for many brands are increasingly reliant upon the scale and depth of the data they collect on consumers. But trust is a fickle thing, as some brands are starting to learn to their cost, and the way in which privacy is managed is becoming a point of differentiation.

Brands need to start exploring this space rather than sitting on their hands and hoping for the best. It is only by exploring this area that the boundaries will become clear. And in fact, having a more open dialogue with consumers may well even engender greater trust and openness to the extent that they may be willing to offer personal data from other sources if they can see that brands are using it in a responsible manner that offers value.

Notes

1 Strong, Colin (2013) Do teenagers actually care about online privacy? Mediatel Newsline, 21 August [online] http://mediatel. co.uk/newsline/2013/08/21/do-teenagers-actually-care-about-online-privacy/

2 Strong, Colin (2013) Five things you may not know about teenagers and privacy, *Huffington Post*, 21 August [online] http://www.huffing tonpost.co.uk/colin-strong/five-things-you-may-not-know-about-teen agers-and-privacy_b_3785248.html

3 Zuckerberg, Mark (2010) Facebook's Zuckerberg says privacy no longer a 'social norm', *Huffington Post*, 18 March [online] http://www. huffingtonpost.com/2010/01/11/facebooks-zuckerberg-the_n_417969. html

4 Madden, Mary, Lenhart, Amanda, Cortesi, Sandra, Gasser, Urs, Duggan, Mary, Smith, Aaron and Beaton, Meredith (2013) Teens, Social Media and Privacy, *Pew Research Centre* [online] http://www. pewinternet.org/Reports/2013/Teens-Social-Media-And-Privacy.aspx

5 Henley, Jon (2013) Are teenagers really careless about online privacy? *The Guardian*, 21 October [online] http://www.theguardian.com/tech nology/2013/oct/21/teenagers-careless-about-online-privacy

6 Boyd, Dana and Marwick, Alice (2011) Social steganography: privacy in 'networked' publics, Paper presented at ICA on 28 May 2011 in Boston, MA

7 Acquisti, Alessandro (2014) The economics and behavioural economics of privacy, in Lane, Julia, Stodden, Victoria, Bender, Stefan and Nissenbaum, Helen (eds) *Privacy, Big Data, and the Public Good: Frameworks for engagement*, Cambridge University Press

8 Calo, Ryan (2011) The boundaries of privacy harm, *Indiana Law Journal*, 86, pp 1131–62

9 Acquisti, Alessandro (2014) (see note 7 above)

10 Acquisti, Alessandro and Grossklags, Jens (2006) What can behavioural economics teach us about privacy? Draft preliminary version, presented as Keynote Paper at ETRICS 2006, available online at http://www.heinz.cmu.edu/~acquisti/papers/Acquisti-Grossklags-Chapter-Etrics.pdf

11 Acquisti, Alessandro, John, Leslie and Lowenstein, George (2013) What is privacy worth? *The Journal of Legal Studies* **42** (2), pp 249–74

12 Brandimarte, Laura, Acquisti, Alessandro and Lowenstein, George (2013) Misplaced confidences, privacy and the control paradox, *Social Psychological and Personality Science* **4** (3), pp 340–47

13 Cukier, Kenneth and Mayer-Schönberger, Viktor (2013) *Big Data: A revolution that will transform how we live, work and think*, John Murray

14 Fournier, Susan (1998) Consumers and their brands: developing relationship theory in consumer research, *Journal of Consumer Research* **24** (4), pp 343–53

15 Aaker, Jennifer, Fournier, Susan and Brasel, S Adam (2004) When good brands do bad, *Journal of Consumer Research*, pp 1–16, 31 June

16 Strong, Colin (2013) Are consumers finally getting interested in terms and conditions? *Huffington Post*, 21 May [online] http://www.huffingtonpost.co.uk/colin-strong/are-consumers-interested-terms-and-conditions_b_3242411.html

17 Ctrl-Shift (2014) Trust Frameworks: Driving privacy and growth, [online] https://www.ctrl-shift.co.uk/research/product/86

18 Federal Trade Commission (2012) Protecting consumer privacy in an era of rapid change: recommendations for businesses and policy makers [online] http://www.ftc.gov/os/2012/03/120326privacyreport.pdf

19 The White House (2012) Consumer data privacy in networked world [online] http://www.whitehouse.gov/sites/default/files/privacy-final.pdf

20 Reitman, Rainey (2012) FTC final privacy report draws a map to meaningful privacy protection in the online world, Electronic Frontier Foundation [online] https://www.eff.org/deeplinks/2012/03/ftc-final-privacy-report-draws-map-meaningful-privacy-protection-online-world

21 Adjerid, Idris, Acquisti, Alessandro, Brandimarte, Laura and Loewenstein, George (2013) Sleights of privacy: framing, disclosures, and the limits of transparency. Published in SOUPS *13 Proceedings of the Ninth Symposium on Usable Privacy and Security* Article No. 9

22 Thaler, Richard, and Sunstein, Cass (2008) *Nudge: Improving decisions about health, wealth, and happiness*, Yale University Press

FINAL THOUGHTS

So at the end of this book it's a fair question to ask, 'what do I think?' Whilst the book has aimed to steer a balanced path through the debate, it's perhaps useful to give my views on what all this means for the different stakeholder groups engaged in big data.

Just how useful is big data to marketers?

As set out at the beginning of the book, the debate around big data has become polarized between the technologists and the sceptics. In my mind, both the extremes of these positions have got it wrong.

First, the case against the 'technologists', those that believe that technology alone is the solution to understanding human behaviour and driving marketing activity. In my mind the technologists are guilty of overstating the case for big data. It is clear from the analysis set out in this book that our ability to predict individual behaviour is limited and, linked to this, the jury is out in the case for personalized advertising. The implications of this for much of the burgeoning big data analytics and indeed programmatic advertising industries are huge. Many brands are putting big bets on the success of these very activities as means of finding growth and profitability in their markets. Whilst there are clearly benefits to be generated from the type of big data analytics commonly practised to date, the scale of opportunity has been over-stated.

Technologists also tend to have a pretty gung-ho attitude to the quality of data that they encounter. Surely 'big' compensates for the messiness of the data, or so the argument goes. But whilst the arrival of the new means it is tempting to think that old rules do not apply, it is increasingly clear that many of the same principles apply to big data as to small data. We still need to question its representativeness, understand the subjective nature of the way we clean the data, avoid the pitfalls in the interpretation process and so on. Of course there are things that are different, new opportunities arise, new tools are required but we cannot ignore the principles that have guided data analysis for many, many years.

So now the case against the sceptics, those that believe that big data does not represent a step change for marketers. The sceptics' position has been bolstered by the way in which the enthusiasm and blanket media coverage of big data has led to an inevitable backlash. But to reject this new phenomenon out of hand would be a huge mistake.

First, at a very simple level, we are now able to observe behaviours that we were never able to do before with any real confidence of accuracy. We can now see the time of day, location, frequency and context of when I purchase my breakfast cereal. Or my transport activities, my banking behaviour, fitness levels and so on. To marketers, even having this basic detail is an absolute gold mine. And indeed, much of the current big data activity is involved in exploring exactly this. This data which seems pretty unexciting to many, is hugely valuable for marketers.

Second, and in my mind more importantly, we are starting to see the development of new ways of interpreting data that allow us to develop much more sophisticated ways of understanding consumers. So we are moving away from simply tracking behavioural data to identifying a much more nuanced understanding of individuals and their relationships with each other. As brands seek to find new ways of understanding and engaging with consumers, this is an area that has huge potential.

It is important to note that this is fundamentally different to the current big data agenda. The current sentiment is all about understanding fairly simplistic information about individual behaviours, lifestyle, life stage etc, so that advertising can be more effectively targeted. What the new agenda in big data is about is delivering a better understanding of the way in which individuals and markets work. It is less about trying to 'predict and control' and more about 'measure and react' strategies. This requires more confidence from marketers to then leap from the data to business strategy but my sense is that this will be welcomed by marketers who are typically well equipped to make sensible judgements from data.

Big marketing

Implicit throughout this book has been a call for marketing to take back the reins of their profession from the technologists. Of course the technologists' approach to marketing is able to tell a good ROI story. But at what cost to the long-term health of the brand? The highly reductionist approach advocated by those taking a very data-centric slant will have little of value to say, for example, about the positioning of the brand. And it will struggle to identify what customers might like that no one is currently offering. Data will only take us so far along the journey and, at some point, human intervention is needed.

Hybrid approaches are needed where we take the positives from different approaches and meld them together. And this is really what this book has been about – marketing is the key to deriving value from big data but needs to get better at leveraging three areas to do so:

- **Social science:** Business needs to get more comfortable with using theoretical frameworks to help explain consumer behaviour. The increasing popularity for brands of behavioural economics and related disciplines certainly suggests that there is an increasing willingness to engage with 'theory'. Of course, the challenge is to find a new breed of consumer researchers and marketers that can translate these explanatory frameworks into a language that can be understood in a business environment and more importantly, deploy it in a way that improves business performance.

- **Consumer insights:** We can only disentangle the 'signal from the noise' by understanding the nuances of consumer behaviour. Otherwise, simply using statistical significance rather than 'colloquial significance' will lead to all manner of erroneous conclusions. And this understanding is of course partly through market research but also through ensuring that the task of understanding consumers is not just the mandate of a centralized team. Huge amounts of valuable, nuanced understanding resides throughout the structure of an organization. Better use needs to be made of this.

- **Data analytics**: This is where the above two areas are deployed to generate insight. Brands often have huge amounts of data at their disposal but frequently do not know 'what to do with it'. As this book sets out, there are big opportunities for brands to apply this new agenda to their data assets. And this is not to say that there is no longer a role for traditional market research techniques but a reassessment needs to be made of how and where they should be deployed as the action moves to examining the insights that can be derived from data already in the hands of the organization.

But just how can a brand organize itself to work in this way? What are the key considerations that should be made to deliver on 'Big Marketing'. My thoughts on this are set out below.

Data due diligence

It is clear that one of the key challenges is for brands to take an intelligent approach to the way in which they critically examine their data assets. I don't think that many organizations have yet properly adjusted their processes for big data sets – a more coherent approach is often required.

The key actions that brands can undertake include:

- Develop processes to determine the provenance of the data, to establish its representativeness and understand the degree to which conclusions can be applied across different business issues. Market researchers are often good at this, having had long experience of designing representative samples from a wide variety of populations.

- Develop frameworks of thinking to help guide the analysis process, as outlined in Chapter 3. Most organizations are drowning in data but at the same time can find themselves taking a fairly tactical approach to analytics of their data assets. Adopting these sorts of frameworks will help to disentangle the different types of analytics so encouraging a more strategic approach to the data analytics process.

- Deploy psychologists to help the business frame the questions and guide the analytics process. There are many traps lying in wait for the unsuspecting data analyst who has usually not been exposed to the nuances of how our minds can so easily lead us in the wrong direction. Big investment decisions are made on analytics so all measures should be taken so that traps are side-stepped.

- Make a distinction between data factory and data lab. The factory needs to be driving much of the basic behavioural reporting that is needed for the day to day of the organization's marketing imperatives. The lab is where new insights are created. Too often these different requirements are confused so neither is done well.

Driving insights from data

Once a brand has processes in place that undertake the 'due diligence' on the way in which data assets are being handled, we can focus on the actions required to drive insight from the data. To this end, it is clear that the following should be considered:

- Make full use of social science to guide analysis of the big data assets. Build relationships with academic institutions to access the thinking that will generate differentiation. A new breed of business-oriented social scientists are emerging who can effectively bridge the gap between academia and business – find these people and deploy them in the business.

- Involve the consumer insights team. Too often (although this is changing) the team responsible for data analytics employs very numerate data scientists, but typically no one who has a nuanced understanding of the consumer themself. If brands are to achieve full value from their data assets this clearly has to change.

- Involve a broad range of stakeholders. It is amazing just how often the answer to a business issue lies in the understanding and creativity of an employee within the business. Develop programmes that are effective in engaging them or consulting with them in the analysis process.

Understanding the consumer experience

A core theme of the book has been that where humans are involved, things can get complicated. It is so much easier for us to assume that humans will behave in predictable, rational and linear ways but, as the findings outlined in Part Three demonstrate, our reactions to living and working in data-mediated environments are not necessarily what might always be expected. The problem is, get this wrong and you can destroy so much built up trust in a very short space of time. So, what should brands do? My recommendations are to:

- Make sure you keep the consumers' best interests at your heart when it comes to how you treat their personal data. Easy to say but harder to do when your business model might involve, for example, maximizing disclosure from consumers. Examine your company's processes and ask if you can honestly say that your customers are best served by your practices. Do your customers think you have their best interests at heart? History suggests that to fail to do so will ultimately, at some point, be a brand's downfall.

- Research the reality of the consumer experience of a data-mediated world. What is it actually like to receive targeted advertising, to have tailored customer service, to have to make decisions concerning your privacy? These are complex issues which will vary by market category and consumer segment but nevertheless understanding is essential if a brand is to ensure that the data investments are maximized and not dashed by a lack of empathy of how they will be received.

Finally

There is a huge amount written about big data and the way in which brands should respond to its promises and threats. However, much of what is written often has an implicit assumption about humans. This effectively considers that an appropriate metaphor for humans is that of a poor quality computer. What I have attempted to do in this book is challenge this assumption and demonstrate that a much richer and more nuanced view of humans and our consumer behaviour is possible and indeed extended through an intelligent analysis and use of data. Brands that choose to explore how this can apply to their own business create the opportunity to generate real value and differentiation from big data.

INDEX

The index is filed in alphabetical, word-by-word order. 'Mc' is filed as spelt in full and acronyms are filed as presented. Page locators in *italics* denote information contained within a figure or table; locators as roman numerals denote material contained within the Preface.

CPSIA information can be obtained at www.ICGtesting.com
Printed in the USA
BVOW11s1211241215

430975BV00010B/43/P